Bountiful Bites

Complete Recipes for Abundant Meals

By

Laura W. McMillin

BREAD, AND BREAKFAST CAKES.

It requires experience to make good bread. One must know, first, how long to let the bread rise, as it takes a longer time in cold than in warm weather; second, when the oven is just of proper temperature to bake it. Bread should be put in a rather hot oven. It is nearly light enough to bake when put in; so the rule for baking bread differs from that of baking cake, which should be put into a moderate oven at first, to become equally heated through before rising. As bread requires a brisk heat, it is well to have the loaves small, the French-bread loaves being well adapted to a hot oven. After the bread is baked, the loaves should be placed on end (covered) at the back of the table until they become cool.

To Make Yeast.

Ingredients: A cupful of baker's yeast; four cupfuls of flour; two large potatoes, boiled; one cupful of sugar, and six cupfuls of boiling water.

Mix the warm mashed potatoes and sugar together; then add the flour; next, add the six cupfuls of boiling water, poured on slowly: this cooks the flour a little. It will be of the consistency of batter. Let the mixture get almost cold, stirring it well, that the bottom may become cool also. It will spoil the yeast if the batter be too hot. When lukewarm, add the tea-cupful of yeast. Leave this mixture in the kitchen, or in some warm place, perhaps on the kitchen-table (do not put it too near the stove), for five or six hours, until it gets perfectly light. Do not touch it until it gets somewhat light; then stir it down two or three times during the six hours. This process makes it stronger. Keep it in a cool place until needed.

This yeast will last perpetually, if a tea-cupful of it be always kept, when making bread, to make new yeast at the next baking. Keep it in a stone jar, scalding the jar every time fresh yeast is made.

In summer, it is well to mix corn-meal with the yeast, and dry it in cakes, in some shady, dry place, turning the cakes often, that they may become thoroughly dry. It requires about one and a half cakes (biscuit-cutter) to make four medium-sized loaves of bread. Crumb them, and let them soak in lukewarm water about a quarter or half an hour before using.

To make the Bread.

Ingredients: Flour, one and a half cupfuls of yeast, lukewarm water, a table-spoonful of lard, a little salt.

Put two quarts of flour into the bread-bowl; sprinkle a little salt over it; add one and a half cupfuls of yeast, and enough lukewarm water to make it a rather soft dough. Set it one side to rise. In winter, it will take overnight; in summer, about three hours. After it has risen, mix well into it one table-spoonful of lard; then add flour (not too much), and knead it half an hour. The more it is kneaded, the whiter and finer it becomes. Leave this in the bread-bowl for a short time to rise; then make it into loaves. Let it rise again for the third time. Bake.

Mrs. Bonner's Bread.

This is a delicious bread, which saves the trouble of making yeast. Twenty-five cents' worth of Twin Brothers' yeast will last a small family six weeks. I would recommend Mrs. Bonner's bread in preference to that of the last receipt. It is cheaper and better, at last, to always have good bread, which is insured by using fresh yeast each time.

For four loaves: At noon, boil three potatoes; mash them well; add a little salt, and two and a half cupfuls of flour; also enough boiling water (that in which the potatoes were boiled) to make rather a thin batter. Let it cool, and when it is at about blood-heat, add a Twin Brothers' yeast-cake, soaked in half a tea-cupful of lukewarm water. One yeast-cake will be sufficient for four loaves of bread in summer; but use one and a half yeast-cakes in winter. Stir well, and put it in a warm place. At night it will be light, when stir in enough flour to make the sponge. Do not make it too stiff. If you should happen to want a little more bread than usual, add a little warm water to the batter. Let it remain in a warm place until morning, when it should be well kneaded for at least twenty minutes. Half an hour or more would be better. Return the dough to the pan, and let it rise again. When light, take it out; add half a tea-spoonful of soda, dissolved in a table-spoonful of water; separate it into four loaves; put them in the pans, and let it rise again. When light, bake it an hour.

French Bread (*Grace Melaine Lourant*).

Put a heaping table-spoonful of hops and a quart of hot water over the fire to boil. Have ready five or six large boiled potatoes, which mash fine. Strain the hops. Now put a pint of boiling water (that in which the potatoes were boiled) over three cupfuls of flour; mix in the mashed potatoes, then the quart of strained hot hop-water, a heaping tea-spoonful of sugar, and the same of salt. When this is lukewarm, mix in one and a half Twin Brothers' yeast-cakes (softened). Let this stand overnight in a warm place.

In the morning, a new process is in order: First, pour over the yeast a table-spoonful of warm water, in which is dissolved half a spoonful of soda; mix in lightly about ten and a half heaping tea-cupfuls of sifted flour. No more flour is added to the bread during its kneading. Instead, the hands are wet in lukewarm water. Now knead the dough, giving it about eight or ten strokes; then taking it from the side next to you, pull it up into a long length, then double it, throwing it down *snappishly* and heavily. Wetting the hands again, give it the same number of strokes, or *kneads*, pulling the end toward you again, and throwing it over the part left in the pan. Continue this process until large bubbles are formed in the dough. It will take half an hour or longer. The hands should be wet enough at first to make the dough rather supple. If dexterously managed, it will not stick to the hands after a few minutes; and when it is kneaded enough, it will be very elastic, full of bubbles, and will not stick to the pan. When this time arrives, put the dough away again in a warm place to rise. This will take one or two hours.

Now comes another new process. Sprinkle plenty of flour on the board, and take out lightly enough dough to make one loaf of bread, remembering that the French loaves are not large, nor of the same shape as the usual home-made ones. With the thumb and forefinger gather up the sides carefully (to prevent doubling the meshes or grain of the dough) to make it round in shape. Flour the rolling-pin, press it in the centre, rolling a little to give the dough the form of cut.

Now give each puffed end a roll toward the centre, lapping well the ends. Turn the bread entirely over, pulling out the ends a little, to give the loaf a long form, as in cut.

Sprinkle plenty of flour on large baking-pans turned bottom side up, upon which lay this and the other loaves, a little distance apart, if there is room for two of them on one pan. Sprinkle plenty of flour on the tops, and set the pans by the side of the fire to again rise a little. It will take twenty-five or thirty minutes longer. Then bake.

Kneading bread in the manner just described causes the *grain* of the bread to run in one direction, so that it may be pealed off in layers. Kneading with water instead of flour makes the bread moist and elastic, rather than solid and in crumbs.

Petits Pains

are made as in last receipt, by lightly gathering a little handful of dough, picking up the sides, and turning it over in the form of a ball or a biscuit. They are baked as described for French bread, placing them a little distance apart, so that they may be separate little breads, each one enough for one person at breakfast.

Toast.

I have remarked before that not one person in a thousand knows how to make good toast. The simplest dishes seem to be the ones oftenest spoiled. If the cook sends to the table a properly made piece of toast, one may judge that she is a *scientific* cook, and may entertain, at the same time, exalted hopes of her.

The bread should not be too fresh. It should be cut *thin*, evenly, and in good shape. The crust edges should be cut off. The pieces shaved off can be dried and put in the bread-crumb can. The object of toasting bread is to extract all its moisture—to convert the dough into pure farina of wheat, which is very digestible. Present each side of the bread to the fire for a few moments to *warm*, without attempting to toast it; then turn about the first side at some distance from the fire, so that it may slowly and evenly receive a *golden* color all over the surface. Now turn it to the other side, moving it in the same way, until it is perfectly toasted. The coals should be clear and hot. Serve it the moment it is done, on a warm plate, or, what is better, a toast-rack; consequently, do not have a piece of bread toasted until the one for whom it is intended is ready to eat it.

"If, as is generally done, a thick slice of bread is hurriedly exposed to a hot fire, and the exterior of the bread is toasted nearly black, the intention of extracting the moisture is defeated, as the heat will then produce no effect on the interior of the slice, which remains as moist as ever. Charcoal is a bad conductor of heat. The overtoasted surface is nothing more or less than a thin layer of charcoal, which prevents the heat from penetrating through the bread. Neither will butter pass through the hard surface: it will remain on it, and if exposed to heat, to melt it in, it will dissolve, and run over it in the form of rancid oil. *This* is why buttered toast is so often unwholesome."

DIXIE BISCUIT (*Mrs. Blair*).

Mix one tea-spoonful of salt into three pints of flour; put one tea-cupful of milk, with two table-spoonfuls of lard, on the fire to warm. Pour this on two eggs, well beaten; add the flour, with one tea-cupful of home-made yeast. When well mixed, set it in a warm place for about five hours to rise; then form into biscuit; let them rise again. Bake.

GRAHAM BREAD.

Make the sponge as for white bread; then knead in Graham flour, only sifting part of it. Add, also, two or three table-spoonfuls of molasses.

RUSKS.

Add to about a quart of bread dough the beaten yolks of three eggs, half a cupful of butter, and one cupful of sugar: mix all well together. When formed into little cakes (rather high and slender, and placed very near each other), rub the tops with sugar and water mixed; then sprinkle over dry sugar. This should fill two pans.

PARKER HOUSE ROLLS (*Mrs. Samuel Treat*).

Ingredients: Two quarts of flour, one pint of milk (measured after boiling), butter the size of an egg, one table-spoonful of sugar, one tea-cupful of home-made yeast, and a little salt.

Make a hole in the flour. Put in the other ingredients, in the following order: sugar, butter, milk, and yeast. Do not stir the ingredients after putting them together. Arrange this at ten o'clock at night; set it in a cool place until ten o'clock the next morning, when mix all together, and knead it fifteen minutes by the clock. Put it in a cool place again until four o'clock P.M., when cut out the rolls, and set each one apart from its neighbor in the pan. Set it for half an hour in a warm place. Bake fifteen minutes.

BEATEN BISCUIT.

Rub one quarter of a pound of lard into one and a half pounds of flour, adding a pinch of salt. Mix enough milk or water with it to make a *stiff* dough. Beat the dough well with a rolling-pin for half an hour or more, or until the dough will *break* when pulled. Little machines come for the purpose of making beaten biscuit, which facilitate the operation. Form into little biscuit, prick them on top several times with a fork, and bake.

Soda and Cream of Tartar Biscuit.

Ingredients: One quart of flour, one tea-spoonful of soda, two tea-spoonfuls cream of tartar, one even tea-spoonful of salt, lard or butter the size of a small egg, and milk.

Put the soda, cream of tartar, and salt on the table; mash them smoothly with a knife, and mix well together; mix them as evenly in the flour as possible; then pass it all through the sieve two or three times. The success of the biscuits depends upon the equal distribution of these ingredients. Mix in the lard or butter (melted) as evenly as possible, taking time to rub it between the open hands, to break any little lumps. Now pour in enough milk to make the dough consistent enough to roll out, mixing it lightly with the ends of the fingers. The quicker it is rolled out, cut, and baked, the better will be the biscuits.

The biscuits are cheaper made with cream of tartar and soda than with baking-powder, yet many make the

Biscuits With Baking-powder.

They are made as in the last receipt, merely substituting two heaping tea-spoonfuls of baking-powder for the cream of tartar and soda, and taking the same care to mix evenly.

These biscuits are nice rolled quite thin (half an inch), and cut with a small cutter two inches in diameter. They may be served hot or cold, and are often used at evening companies, cold, split in two, buttered, and with chopped ham (as for sandwiches) placed between them. They are preferable to bread sandwiches, as they do not dry as quickly, and are, perhaps, neater to handle. These biscuits are especially nice when made with Professor Horsford's self-raising flour—of course, the raising powders are omitted. The appreciation of hot biscuits is quite a Southern and Western American fancy. They are rarely seen abroad, and are generally considered unwholesome in the Eastern States.

Muffins.

Ingredients: Two eggs, one pint of flour, one tea-cupful of milk or cream, butter half the size of an egg, a little salt, and one tea-spoonful of baking-powder.

Mix the baking-powder and salt in the flour. Beat the eggs; add to the yolks, first, milk, then butter (melted), then flour, then the whites. Beat well after it is all mixed, and bake them immediately in a hot oven, in gem-pans or rings. Take them out of the pans or rings the moment they are done, and send them to the table. The self-raising flour is very nice for making muffins. In using this, of course, the baking-powder should be omitted.

Waffles.

Ingredients: Two eggs, one pint of flour, one and a quarter cupfuls of milk or cream, one even tea-spoonful of yeast-powder, butter or lard the size of a walnut, and salt.

Mix the baking-powder and salt well in the flour, then rub in evenly the butter; next add the beaten yolks and milk mixed, then the beaten whites of the eggs. Bake immediately.

Rice Waffles (*Mrs. Gratz Brown*).

Ingredients: One and a half pints of boiled rice, one and a half pints of flour, half a tea-cupful of sour milk, half a tea-cupful of sweet milk, one tea-spoonful of soda, salt, three eggs, and butter size of a walnut.

Rice Pancakes

are made as in the last receipt, by adding an extra half-cupful of milk.

Hominy Cake (*Mrs. Watts Sherman*).

Add a spoonful of butter to two cupfuls of whole hominy (boiled an hour with milk) while it is still hot. Beat three eggs very light, which add to the hominy. Stir in gradually a pint of milk, and, lastly, a pint of corn-meal. Bake in a pan.

This is a very nice breakfast cake. Serve it, with a large napkin under it, on a plate. The sides of the napkin may cover the top of the cake until the moment of serving, which will keep it moist.

Baked Hominy Grits (*Mrs. Pope*).

Ingredients: One quart of milk, one cupful of hominy grits, two eggs, and salt.

When the milk is salted and boiling, stir in the hominy grits, and boil for twenty minutes. Set it aside to cool thoroughly. Beat the eggs to a stiff froth, and then beat them well and hard into the hominy. Bake half an hour.

Breakfast Puffs, or Pop-overs (*Mrs. Hopkins*).

Ingredients: Two cupfuls of milk, two cupfuls of flour, two eggs, and an even tea-spoonful of salt.

Beat the eggs separately and well, add the whites last, and then beat all well together. They may be baked in roll-pans, or deep gem-pans, which should be heated on the range, and greased before the batter is put in: they should be filled half full with the batter. Or they may be baked in tea-cups, of which eight would be required for this quantity of batter. When baked, serve immediately. For Graham gems use half Graham flour.

Henriettes for Tea (*French Cook*), No. 1.

Ingredients: Three eggs beaten separately, three-fourths of a cupful of cream or milk, a scant tea-spoonful of baking-powder, salt, one table-spoonful of brandy, a pinch of cinnamon, enough flour to make them just stiff enough to roll out easily.

Roll them thin as a wafer, cut them into about two-inch squares, or into diamonds, with the paste-jagger, fry them in boiling lard, and sprinkle over pulverized sugar.

Henriettes for Breakfast or Tea (*French Cook*), No. 2.

Ingredients: Three eggs beaten separately, one cupful of milk, a scant tea-spoonful of baking-powder, salt, one table-spoonful of brandy, and flour enough to make a little thicker than for pancakes.

Pass the batter through a funnel (one-third or one-half inch diameter at end) into hot boiling lard, making rings, or any figures preferred. Do not fry too much at one time. When done and drained, sprinkle over pulverized sugar, and lay them on a plate on a folded napkin. Serve.

Wafer Biscuits.

Rub a piece of butter the size of a large hickory-nut into a pint of sifted flour; sprinkle over a little salt. Mix it into a stiff, smooth paste, with the white of an egg beaten to a froth, and warm milk. Beat the paste with a rolling-pin for half an hour, or longer; the more the dough is beaten, the better are the biscuits. Form the dough into little round balls about the size of a pigeon's egg; then roll each of them to the size of a saucer. They should be mere wafers in thickness; they can not be too thin. Sprinkle a little flour over the tins. Bake.

These wafers are exceedingly nice to serve with a cheese course, or for invalids to eat with their tea.

CORN BREAD.

Ingredients: One cupful of sour milk, one cupful of sweet milk, one table-spoonful of sugar or molasses, one tea-cupful of flour, two heaping tea-cupfuls of corn-meal, one tea-spoonful of salt, one tea-spoonful (not heaping) of soda, one and a half table-spoonfuls of melted lard or butter, and three eggs.

Beat the eggs separately; add the melted butter to the milk; then the sugar, salt, yolks, soda (dissolved in a table-spoonful of warm water); and, lastly, the whites, flour, and corn-meal. Beat it all quickly and well together. Put it immediately in the oven, to bake half an hour.

HOE CAKE.

Pour enough scalding water, or milk, on corn-meal (salted), to make it rather moist. Let it stand an hour, or longer. Put two or three heaping table-spoonfuls on a hot griddle, greased with pork or lard. Smooth over the surface, making the cake about half an inch thick, and of round shape. When browned on one side, turn and brown it on the other. Serve very hot.

These are very nice breakfast cakes, with a savory crust.

CORN CAKE (*Mrs. Lackland*).

Ingredients: One pint of milk, half a pint of Indian meal, four eggs, a scant table-spoonful of butter, salt, and one tea-spoonful of sugar. Pour the milk boiling on the *sifted* meal. When cold, add the butter (melted), the salt, the sugar, the yolks of the eggs, and, lastly, the whites, well beaten separately. Bake half an hour in a hot oven. It is very nice baked in iron or tin gem-pans, the cups an inch and a half deep.

FRIED CORN MUSH FOR BREAKFAST.

Many slice the mush when cold, and simply *sauté* it in a little hot lard. But as some cooks seem to have as great success in simple dishes as in elaborate ones, I shall consider this as at least one of the little successes taught me by a French cook. Of course, the mush is made by sprinkling the corn-meal into *boiling salted* water, or after the manner of Harriet Plater, given in the next receipt. It is thoroughly cooked, and made the day before wanted. When cold, it is sliced, each slice dipped in beaten eggs (salted) and bread or cracker crumbs, and fried in boiling-hot lard. One should try this, to know the superiority in the manner of cooking.

CORN MUSH

is usually made by sprinkling corn-meal into well-salted boiling water (a pint of corn-meal to three pints of water), and cooking it well. But Harriet Plater (Mrs. Filley's most skillful cook) says that corn-meal mush is much lighter, and when fried for breakfast, browns better by cooking it as follows:

"Put a quart of water on the fire to boil. Stir a pint of cold milk, with one pint of corn-meal and one tea-spoonful of salt. When the water boils, pour in the mixture gradually, stirring all well together. Let it boil for half an hour, stirring often, to prevent it from burning."

OATMEAL PORRIDGE.

It seems very simple to make oatmeal porridge, yet it is a very different dish made by different cooks. The ingredients are: One heaping cupful of oatmeal to one quart of boiling water and one tea-spoonful of salt. Boil twenty minutes.

The water should be salted and boiling when the meal is sprinkled in with one hand, while it is lightly stirred in with the other. When all mixed, it should boil without afterward being stirred more than is necessary to keep it from burning at the bottom, and to mingle the grains two or three times, so that they may all be evenly cooked. If much stirred, the porridge will be starchy or waxy, and poor in flavor. But the puffing of the steam through the grains without much stirring swells each one separately, and, when done, the porridge is light, and quite consistent. This same manner of cooking is applicable as well to all other grains.

MOTHER JOHNSON'S PANCAKES (*Adirondacks*).

These are famous pancakes, and, like every other good thing, there is a little secret in the preparation.

Enough flour is added to a quart of sour milk to make a rather thick batter. The secret is that it is left to stand overnight, instead of being finished at once. It may even stand to advantage for twenty-four hours. However, if it is mixed at night, the next morning two well-beaten eggs and salt are to be added at the same time with half a tea-spoonful of soda, dissolved in a table-spoonful of warm water. Cook immediately.

Sirup.

Mix two table-spoonfuls of water to two cupfuls of brown sugar and one even table-spoonful of butter. Let it boil about five minutes.

Buckwheat Cakes.

Scald two gills of Indian meal in one quart of boiling water. Add a little salt. When cool, add one gill of yeast, and stir in enough buckwheat flour to make a thin batter. Let it rise overnight. If by chance it is a little sour, just before cooking add one-fourth of a tea-spoonful of soda, dissolved in half a cupful of boiling water. Or,

They may be made in the same manner without the Indian meal, merely adding the yeast to a quart of lukewarm water, and making the batter with buckwheat flour alone.

Pancakes, with Flour or Corn-meal.

Stir one or two cupfuls of cream or milk into two beaten eggs; add flour or corn-meal enough to make a thin batter. If the milk is sweet, add one tea-spoonful of yeast-powder; if it is sour, add, instead of the yeast-powder, half a tea-spoonful of soda, dissolved in a little warm water.

Pancakes, with Bread-crumbs.

Soak the bread-crumbs, then drain them. To two cupfuls of bread-crumbs add one cupful of flour or corn-meal, one egg, and milk enough to make a thin batter. If the milk is sweet, add a tea-spoonful of yeast-powder; if sour, half a tea-spoonful of soda, dissolved in a table-spoonful of warm water.

Strawberry Short-cake (*Mrs. Pope*).

Ingredients: One quart of flour, two heaping tea-spoonfuls of yeast-powder, half a tea-spoonful of salt, butter size of an egg, milk, two quarts of strawberries. Mix the baking-powder into the flour, then rub in the butter (in the same manner as described for biscuits, page 72). Add enough milk to make a soft dough—rather softer than for biscuits. Spread this on two pie-tins. Bake in a quick oven.

When the cakes are done, let them partly cool. Cut around the edges, and split them. Spread them with butter, then with one quart of mashed strawberries, with plenty of sugar; then put between them the other quart of whole strawberries, sprinkled with sugar. Serve a pitcher of cream with a strawberry short-cake. The cake in this form can be cut like a pie. It is a good summer breakfast as well as tea dish. Or,

It can be made with sour milk, viz.: to two tea-cupfuls of sour milk add a tea-spoonful of soda, then three-fourths of a tea-cupful of butter or lard, partly melted, and enough flour to make a soft dough. Roll it into thin cakes large enough to fill the pan in which they are to be baked. When baked, split, and butter them while hot. Lay on a plate half of the cake, put on a layer of well-sugared strawberries, then the other half, then more strawberries, and so on, until there are several layers. Or,

These cakes can be made in the same way with currants, blackberries, cut peaches, chopped pine-apples, raspberries, etc.

TEA.

Two things are necessary to insure good tea: first, that the water should be at the boiling-point when poured on the leaves, water simply hot not answering the purpose at all; and, second, that it should be served freshly made. Tea should never be boiled. So particular are the English to preserve its first aroma, that it is sometimes made on the table two or three times during a meal. In France, little silver canisters of tea are placed on the table, where it is invariably made. One tea-spoonful of the leaves is a fair portion for each person. Tea is better made in an earthen tea-pot, which tea connoisseurs are particular to have. They also drink the beverage without milk, and with loaf-sugar merely.

Water at the first boiling-point is generally considered better for tea or coffee, and, in fact, any kind of cooking which requires boiling water.

COFFEE.

The best coffee is made by mixing two-thirds Java and one-third Mocha. The Java gives strength, the Mocha flavor and aroma.

Coffee should be evenly and carefully roasted. Much depends upon this. If even a few of the berries are burned, the coffee will taste burned and bitter, instead of being fine-flavored and aromatic. To have the perfection of coffee, it should be fresh-roasted each day. Few, however, will take that trouble. As soon as it is roasted, and while still hot, stir into it one or two eggs, together with their shells (about one egg to a pint of roasted coffee-beans). This will help to preserve the coffee, as well as to make it clear. Put it away in a close-covered tin-case, and grind it only just before using.

Allow two heaping table-spoonfuls of ground coffee to a pint of water. Let the water be *boiling* when it is poured on the coffee. Cover it as tightly as possible, and boil it one minute; then let it remain a few moments at the side of the range to settle.

Delmonico allows one and a half pounds of coffee to one gallon of water. The coffee-pot, with a double base, is placed on the range in a vessel of hot water (*bain-marie*). The boiling water is poured over the coffee, which is contained in a felt strainer in the coffee-pot. It is not boiled.

Of course, much depends upon the care in preparing the coffee to insure a delicious beverage; but equally as much depends upon serving with it good thick cream. Milk, or even boiled milk, is not to be compared with cream. In cities, a gill, at least, might be purchased each morning for coffee, or a few table-spoonfuls might be saved from the evening's milk for at least *one* cup. Fill the cup two-thirds full, then, with hot, clear coffee, pour in one or two table-spoonfuls of cream, and use loaf-sugar.

Professor Blot, in his lectures, was very emphatic as to the impropriety of *boiling* coffee. He said by this means the aroma and flavor were carried into the attic, and a bitter decoction was left to be drunk. He preferred decidedly the coffee made in the French filter coffee-pot.

I have experimented upon coffee, and prefer it boiled for one minute in the ordinary coffee-pot. That made in the French filter is also most excellent. It is not boiled, and requires a greater proportion of coffee. But to be explicit, put the coffee in the filter. At the first boil of the water, pour one or two coffee-cupfuls of it on the coffee. Put back the water on the fire. When boiling again, pour on as much more, and repeat the process until the desired quantity is made.

CHOCOLATE (*Miss Sallie Schenck*).

Allow two sticks of chocolate to one pint of new milk. After the chocolate is scraped, either let it soak an hour or so, with a table-spoonful of milk to soften it, or boil it a few moments in two or three table-spoonfuls of water. Then, in either case, mash it to a smooth paste. When the milk, sweetened to taste with loaf-sugar, is boiling, stir in the chocolate-paste, adding a little of the boiling milk to it first, to dilute it evenly. Let it boil half a minute. Stir it well, or mill it, and serve immediately.

Maillard's chocolate is flavored with a little vanilla. The commoner brands, such as Baker's, will be nearly as good by adding a little vanilla when making. Miss Schenck (noted for her chocolate) adds a very little flavoring of brandy.

A very good addition, and one universally seen, when chocolate is served at lunch parties, is a heaping table-spoonful of whipped-cream, sweetened and flavored with a little vanilla before it is whipped, placed on the top of the chocolate in each cup, the cup being only three-quarters filled with the chocolate.

COCOA.

Many use cocoa rather than chocolate. It has the same flavor, but it has more body, and is richer and more oily. It is made in the same way as chocolate, but a few drops of the essence of vanilla should be invariably added.

SOUP.

The meat should be fresh, lean (all fat possible being removed), and juicy to make the best soup. It is put into cold, clear water, which should be heated only moderately for the first half-hour. The object is to extract the juices of the meat, and if it be boiled too soon, the surface will become coagulated, thereby imprisoning the juice within. After the first half-hour the pot should be placed at the back of the stove, allowing the soup to simmer for four or five hours.

Nothing is more disagreeable at table than greasy soup. As all particles of fat are taken off hot liquor with some difficulty, soup should be made the day before it is to be used, when the fat will rise to the top and harden. It can then be easily removed.

When vegetables are used, they should be added only in time to become thoroughly done: afterward they absorb a portion of the richness of the soup.

When onions are used, they impart better flavor by being fried or *sautéd* in a little hot butter or other grease, before they are added to the soup. In fact, many professional cooks fry other vegetables also, such as carrots and turnips. Sometimes they even fry slightly the chickens, beef, etc., and then cut them into smaller pieces for boiling. Potatoes and cabbage should be boiled in separate water before they are added to a soup.

Amateur cooks seem to have a great aversion to making stock. They think it must be something troublesome, and too scientific to undertake; whereas, in truth, it saves the trouble of going through the process of soup-boiling every day, and it is as easy to make as any simple soup. One has only to increase the quantity of meat and bones to any desired proportion, adding pepper and salt, and also vegetables, if preferred.

The stock should be kept in a stone jar. It will form a jelly, and in cool weather will last at least a week.

Just before dinner each day, in order to prepare soup, it is only necessary to cut off some of the jelly and heat it. It is very good with nothing additional; but one can have a change of soup each day by adding different flavorings, such as onion, macaroni, vermicelli, tomato, tapioca, spring vegetables (which will make a *julienne*), poached eggs, fried bread, asparagus, celery, green pease, etc. I will be explicit about these additions in the receipts. Stock is also valuable for gravies, sauces, and stews, and for boiling many things, such as pigeons, chickens, etc.

Stock, or Pot au Feu.

In ordinary circumstances, beef alone, with some vegetables, will make a good broth or stock, in the proportion of two and a half pints of cold clear water to each pound of bones and meat; the bones and meat should be of about equal weight. It makes the soup more delicate to add chicken or veal. Chicken and veal together make a good soup, called *blond de veau*. Good soup can be made, also, by using the trimmings of fresh meat, bits of cold cooked beef, or the bones of any meat or fowl. In the choice of vegetables, onions (first fried or *sautéd*, and a clove stuck in), parsley, and carrots are oftenest used: turnips, parsnips, and celery should be employed more sparingly. The soup bunch at market is generally a very good distribution of vegetables. Nothing is more simple than the process of making stock or broth. Remember not to let it boil for the first half-hour; then it should simmer slowly and steadily, partly covered, for four or five hours. In royal kitchens the stock is cooked by gas. Skim frequently; as scum, if allowed to remain, gives an unpleasant flavor to the soup. Use salt sparingly, putting in a little at first, and seasoning at the last moment. Many a good soup is spoiled by an injudicious use of seasoning. Some add a few drops of lemon-juice to a broth. If wine or catsup is added, it should only be done at the last moment. Always strain the soup through a sieve or soup-strainer. Small scraps of meat or sediment look slovenly in a soup. Or,

A Simple Stock.

If you have no vegetables (you should always have them, especially onions and carrots, as they will keep), a very good stock can be made by employing the meat and bones alone, seasoned with pepper and salt. If rich enough, it might be served in this manner. However, it is a simple thing, about fifteen minutes before dinner, each day, to add a little boiled macaroni, fried onions, etc., to vary the soup.

Gouffé's Receipt for Stock, or Bouillon.

Three pounds of beef; one pound of bone (about the quantity in that weight of meat); five and a half quarts of clear cold water; two ounces of salt; two carrots, say ten ounces; two large onions, say ten ounces, with two cloves stuck in them; six leeks, say fourteen ounces; one head of celery, say one ounce; two turnips, say ten ounces; one parsnip, say two ounces.

Bouillon Served at Luncheons, Germans, etc.

Purchase about six pounds of beef and bone (soup bones) for ten persons. Cut up the meat and break the bones; add two quarts of cold water, and simmer slowly until all the strength is extracted from the meat. It will take about five hours. Strain it through a fine sieve, removing every particle of fat; and if there is more than ten cupfuls, reduce it by boiling to that quantity. Season only with pepper and salt.

It is served in bouillon cups at luncheons, at evening companies, Germans, etc.

Sometimes it is served clear and transparent, after the receipt for Amber Soup.

Amber Soup, or Clear Broth.

This soup is served at almost all company dinners. There can be no better choice, as a heavy soup is not then desirable.

Ingredients: A large soup bone (say two pounds), a chicken, a small slice of ham, a soup bunch (or an onion, two sprigs of parsley, half a small carrot, half a small parsnip, half a stick of celery), three cloves, pepper, salt, a gallon of cold water, whites and shells of two eggs, and caramel for coloring.

Let the beef, chicken, and ham boil slowly for five hours; add the vegetables and cloves, to cook the last hour, having first fried the onion in a little hot fat, and then in it stuck the cloves. Strain the soup into an earthen bowl, and let it remain overnight. Next day remove the cake of fat on the top; take out the jelly, avoiding the settlings, and mix into it the beaten whites of the eggs with the shells. Boil quickly for half a minute; then, placing the kettle on the hearth, skim off carefully all the scum and whites of the eggs from the top, not stirring the soup itself. Pass this through the jelly bag, when it should be quite clear. The soup may then be put aside, and reheated just before serving. Add then a large table-spoonful of caramel, as it gives it a richer color, and also a slight flavor.

Of course, the brightest and cleanest of kettles should be used. I once saw this transparent soup served in Paris, without color, but made quite thick with tapioca. It looked very clear, and was exceedingly nice.

This soup may be made in one day. After it is strained, add the eggs and proceed as in receipt. However, if it is to be served at a company dinner, it is more convenient to make it the day before.

To make Caramel, or Burned Sugar, for coloring Broth.

The appearance of broth is improved by being of a rich amber color. The most innocent coloring substance, which does not impair the flavor of the broth, is caramel, prepared as follows:

Put into a porcelain saucepan, say half a pound of sugar, and a tablespoonful of water. Stir it constantly over the fire until it has a bright, dark-brown color, being very careful not to let it burn or blacken. Then add a teacupful of water and a little salt; let it boil a few moments longer; cool and strain it. Put it away in a close-corked bottle, and it is always ready for coloring soups.

Thickenings for Soup.

I have before recommended the making of soup the day before it is served, as this is the best means of having it entirely free from fat and settlings. Just before it is served, it may be thickened with corn starch, sago, tapioca, pearl barley, rice, etc. If a thickening of flour is used, let it be a *roux*, mixed according to directions, page 51. However, a rich stock jelly needs no thickening.

Additions To Beef Stock, to form Other Kinds of Soup.

It is well, just before the beef soup is sent to table, to drop into the tureen poached eggs, which have been cooked in salted water, and neatly trimmed. There may be an egg for each person at table. This is a favorite soup in Havana. Or, Put into the tureen, just before the soup is sent to table, slices of lemon—one slice for each plate. Or,

Yolks of hard-boiled eggs, one for each person. Or,

Put into the tureen *croûtons* or dice of bread, say three-quarters of an inch square, fried in a little butter. When frying, or rather *sautéing*, turn them, that all sides may be browned. They may be prepared several hours, if more convenient, before dinner; then left near the fire, to become crisp and dry. This makes a very good soup, and is also an excellent means of using dry bread. It is a favorite French soup, called *potage aux croûtons*. Or,

Drop into the tureen force-meat balls.

Receipt for Force-meat Balls.

Take any kind of meat or chicken, or both (that used for making the soup will answer); chop it very fine; season it with pepper, salt, a little chopped parsley and thyme, or a little parsley and fried onion, or with thyme, or parsley alone, a little lemon-juice, and grated peel. Break in a raw egg, and sprinkle over some flour; roll them in balls the size of a pigeon's egg. Fry or *sauté* them in a little butter, or they may be cooked in boiling water; or they may be egged and bread-crumbed, and fried in boiling lard. This is the most simple receipt. The French take much trouble in making *quenelles*, etc., for soup. Or,

A simple and delicious addition is that of four or five table-spoonfuls of stewed tomatoes.

Macaroni Soup

is only an addition of macaroni to the stock-jelly. However, boil the macaroni first in salted water. When done, drain it, and cut it into about two or three inch lengths. Put these pieces into the soup when it is simmering on the fire, then serve it a few minutes after. Many send, at the same time, a plate of grated cheese. This is passed, a spoon with it, after the plates of soup are served, each person adding a spoonful of it to their soup, if they choose. They probably will not choose it a second time.

Vermicelli Soup

is made exactly as macaroni soup, only the vermicelli is not cut, and, if *very little* of it is used, it may be boiled in the soup. Often the stock for vermicelli is preferred made of veal and chicken, instead of beef; however, either is very good. Grated cheese may also be served with it.

Noodles (*Eleanore Bouillotat*).

Three delicious dishes may be made from this simple and economical receipt for noodles:

To three eggs (slightly beaten), two table-spoonfuls of water, and a little salt, add enough flour to make a rather stiff dough; work it well for fifteen or twenty minutes, as you would dough for crackers, adding flour when necessary. When pliable, cut off a portion at a time, roll it thin as a wafer, sprinkle over flour, and, beginning at one side, roll it into a rather tight roll. With a sharp knife, cut it, from the end, into very thin slices (one-eighth inch), forming little wheels or curls. Let them dry an hour or so. Part may be used to serve as a vegetable, part for a noodle soup, and the rest should be dried, to put one side to use at any time for a beef soup.

To serve as a Vegetable.

Three cupfuls of fresh noodles, three quarts of salted boiling water, bread-crumbs, butter size of an egg.

Throw a few of the noodles at a time into the boiling salted water, and boil them until they are done, separating and shaking them with a large fork to prevent them from matting together. Skin them out when done, and keep them on a warm dish in a warm place until enough are cooked in a similar manner. Now mix the butter (in which the bread-crumbs were fried) evenly in them; put them on the platter on which they are to be served, and sprinkle over the top bread-crumbs fried or *sautéd* in some hot butter until they are of a light-brown color. This is a very good dish to serve with a fish, or with almost any meat, or it can be served as a course by itself; or the noodles can be cooked as macaroni, with cheese.

Noodle Soup.

Add to the water in which the noodles were boiled, as in last receipt, part of the butter in which the bread-crumbs were *sautéd*, a table-spoonful of chopped parsley, and two or three table-spoonfuls of the cooked noodles. Season with more salt, if necessary. Serve.

Beef Noodle Soup.

Add to a beef stock a small handful of fresh or dried noodles about twenty minutes before serving, which will be long enough time to cook them.

Many varieties of soups may be made by adding different kinds of vegetables to beef soup or stock. Cauliflower, cabbage, potatoes, and asparagus are better boiled in separate water, and added to the soup-tureen at the last moment. Onions, leeks, turnips, and carrots are better fried to a light color in a *sauté* pan with a little butter or clarified grease, and added to the soup. In frying, it is better to accompany the vegetable or vegetables with a little onion.

If you add more onion, more turnip, or more carrot than any other vegetable, you have onion, turnip, or carrot soup. I will specify a few combinations of vegetables.

Spring Soup.

A stock with any spring vegetables added which have first been parboiled in other water. Those generally used are pease, asparagus-tops, or a few young onions or leeks. This soup is often colored with caramel. Or,

Here is Francatelli's receipt for spring soup, a little simplified: Cut with a vegetable-cutter two carrots and two turnips into little round shapes; add the white part of a head of celery; twelve small young onions, sliced, without the green stalks; and one head of cauliflower, cut into flowerets. Parboil these vegetables for three minutes in boiling water. Drain, and add them to two quarts of stock, made of chicken or beef (chicken is better). Let the whole simmer gently for half an hour, then add the white leaves of a head-lettuce (cut the size of a half-dollar, with a cutter). As soon as tender, and when about to send the soup to the table, add half a gill of small green pease, and an equal quantity of asparagus-heads, which have been previously boiled in other water.

JULIENNE SOUP, WITH POACHED EGGS (*Dubois*).

Take two medium-sized carrots, a medium-sized turnip, a piece of celery, the core of a lettuce, and an onion. Cut them into thin fillets about an inch long. Fry the onion in butter over a moderate fire, without allowing it to take color; add the carrots, turnips, and celery—raw, if tender; if not, boil them separately for a few minutes. After frying all slowly for a few moments, season with a pinch of salt and a tea-spoonful of powdered-sugar. Then moisten them with a gill of broth, and boil until reduced to a glaze. Now add nearly two quarts of good stock, which has been skimmed and passed through a sieve, and remove the stew-pan to the back of the stove, so that the soup may boil only partially. A quarter of an hour after add the lettuce (which has been boiled in other water), and a few raw sorrel leaves, if they can be procured. This soup is quite good enough without eggs, yet they are a pleasant addition. Poach them in salted water, trim them, and drop into the soup-tureen just as it is ready to send to the table. Many color this soup with caramel. In that case, the sugar should be omitted.

ASPARAGUS SOUP.

Ingredients: Three pints of beef soup or stock, thirty heads of asparagus, a little cream, butter, flour, and a little spinach.

Cut the tops off the asparagus, about half an inch long, and boil the rest. Cut off all the tender portions, and rub them through a sieve, adding a little salt. Warm three pints of stock, add a *roux* made of a small piece of butter and a heaping tea-spoonful of flour; then add the asparagus pulp. Boil it slowly a quarter of an hour, stirring in two or three table-spoonfuls of cream. Color the soup with a tea-spoonful of spinach green, and, just before serving it, add the asparagus-tops, which have been separately boiled.

Many like this soup, but I prefer simply boiled asparagus-points added to stock or beef soup, just before serving.

Spinach Green.

Pound some spinach well, adding a few drops of water; squeeze the juice through a cloth, and put it on a strong fire. As soon as it looks curdy, take it off, and strain the liquor through a sieve. What remains on the sieve will be the coloring matter.

Ox-tail Soup.

Ox-tails make an especially good soup, on account of the gelatinous matter they contain.

Ingredients: Two ox-tails, a soup bunch, or a good-sized onion, two carrots, one stalk of celery, a little parsley, and a small cut of pork.

Cut the ox-tails at the joints, slice the vegetables, and mince the pork. Put the pork into a stew-pan. When hot, add first the onions; when they begin to color, add the ox-tails. Let them fry or *sauté* a very short time. Now cut them to the bone, that the juice may run out in boiling. Put both the ox-tails and fried onions into a soup kettle, with four quarts of cold water. Let them simmer for about four hours; then add the other vegetables, with three cloves stuck in a little piece of onion, and pepper and salt. As soon as the vegetables are well cooked, the soup is done. Strain it. Select some of the joints (one for each plate), trim them, and serve them with the soup. Or, if preferred, the joints may be left out.

Chicken Soup (*Potage à la Reine*).—*Francatelli*.

Roast a large chicken. Clear all the meat from the bones, chop, and pound it thoroughly with a quarter of a pound of boiled rice. Put the bones (broken) and the skin into two quarts of cold water. Let it simmer for some time, when it will make a weak broth. Strain it, and add it to the chicken and rice. Now press this all through a sieve, and put it away until dinner-time. Take off the grease on top; heat it without boiling, and, just before sending to table, mix into it a gill of boiling cream. Season carefully with pepper and salt.

Purée of Chicken (*Giuseppe Romanii*).

Chef de Cuisine of the Cooking-school in New York.

Ingredients: One and a half pounds of chicken, one and a half quarts of white stock (made with veal), half a sprig of thyme, two sprigs of parsley, half a blade of mace, one shallot, a quarter of a pound of rice, and half a pint of cream.

Roast the chicken, and when cold cut off all the flesh; put the bones into the white stock, together with the thyme, mace, parsley, shallot, and washed rice; boil it until the rice is very thoroughly cooked. In the mean time, chop the chicken; pound it in a mortar; then pass it through a sieve or colander, helping the operation by moistening it with a little of the stock. Strain the balance of the stock, allowing the rice to pass through the sieve.

Half an hour before dinner, add the chicken to the stock and heat it *without boiling*. Just before serving, add to it half a pint of boiling cream. Season with pepper and salt.

Plain Chicken Soup.

Cut up the chicken, and break all the bones; put it in a gallon of cold water; let it simmer for five hours, skimming it well. The last hour add, to cook with the soup, a cupful of rice and a sprig of parsley. When done, let the kettle remain quiet a few moments on the kitchen table, when skim off every particle of fat with a spoon. Then pour all on a sieve placed over some deep dish. Take out all the bones, pieces of meat, and parsley. Press the rice through the sieve. Now mix the rice, by stirring it with the soup, until it resembles a smooth *purée*. Season with pepper and salt.

Giblet Soup.

This soup is a great success. It is very inexpensive, a plate of giblets only costing at market five cents. It is a very good imitation of mock-turtle soup, and, after the first experience in making, it will be found very easy to manage.

Ingredients: The giblets of four chickens or two turkeys, one medium-sized onion, one small carrot, half a turnip, two sprigs of parsley, a leaf of sage, eggs, a little lemon-juice, Port or Madeira wine, and one or two cupfuls of chicken or beef stock, quite strong.

Cut up the vegetables. Put a piece of butter the size of a small egg into a stew-pan. When quite hot, throw in the sliced onion. When they begin to brown, add the carrot and turnip, a table-spoonful of flour, and the giblets. Fry them all quickly for a minute, watching them constantly, that the flour may brown, and not burn. Now cut the giblets (that the juice may escape), and put all into the soup-kettle, with a little pepper and salt, and three quarts of water—of course, stock would be much better, and for extra occasions I would recommend it; or without stock, one could add any fresh bones or scraps of lean meat one might happen to have. Pieces of chicken are especially well adapted to this soup; yet, for ordinary occasions, giblets alone answer very well.

Let the soup simmer for five hours; then strain it. Thicken it a little with *roux* (page 51), letting the flour brown, and add to it also one of the livers mashed. Season with the additional pepper and salt it needs, a little lemon-juice, and two table-spoonfuls of Port or Madeira wine. Put into the soup tureen yolks of hard-boiled eggs, one for each person at table. Pour over the soup, and serve.

MOCK-TURTLE SOUP (*New York Cooking-school*).

Let some one beside yourself remove the flesh from a calf's head, viz., cut from between the ears to the nose, touching the bone; then, cutting close to it, take off all the flesh. Turn over the head, cut open the jaw-bone from underneath, and take out the tongue whole. Turn the head back again, crack the top of the skull between the ears, and take out the brains whole; they may be saved for a separate dish. Soak all separately for a few moments in salt and water. Cut the skull all to pieces, wash it quickly, and put it on the fire in four quarts of cold water, together with the flesh, tongue, half a bunch of parsley, half a stalk of celery, one large bay-leaf, three cloves, half an inch of a stick of cinnamon, six whole allspice, six pepper-corns, half of a large carrot, and one turnip. When the tongue is tender, take it out, to be served as a separate dish (with spinach or with *sauce Tartare*). Leave in the flesh for about two hours, when it will be perfectly tender. Let the bones, etc., simmer for six hours, then strain, and put it away until the next day.

At the same time that the calf's head is cooking in one vessel, make a stock in another, with a beef or veal soup-bone (two or three pounds), and any scraps of poultry (it would be improved with a chicken added; and one might take this opportunity to have a boiled chicken for dinner, cooking it in the stock), put into two or three quarts of water, and simmered until reduced to a pint.

The next day, remove the fat and settlings from the two stocks.

Put into a two-quart stew-pan two ounces of butter (size of an egg), and, when it bubbles, stir in an ounce of ham cut in strips, and one heaping table-spoonful of flour (one and a half ounces). Stir it constantly until it gets quite brown, pour the reduced stock over it, mix it well, and strain it.

Now to half a pound of the calf's head cut in dice add one quart of the calf's-head stock boiling hot, and the pint of reduced and thickened stock, the juice of half a lemon, and one glassful of sherry. When it is about to boil, set it one side, and skim it very carefully. Add the flesh cut from the head, cut in dice, and two hard-boiled eggs cut in dice, and salt. Or,

Receipt for Egg-balls.—If, instead of the egg-dice, egg-balls should be preferred, add to the yolks of two hard-boiled eggs the raw yolk of one egg, one table-spoonful of melted butter, a little salt and pepper, and enough sifted flour to make it consistent enough to handle. Sprinkle flour on the board, roll it out about half an inch thick, cut it into dice, and roll each one into little balls in the palm of the hand. Put these into the soup five minutes before it is served, to cook. Or,

Receipt for Meat-balls.—If, instead of meat-dice, meat-balls should be preferred, to three-fourths of a cupful of the head-meat, chopped very fine, add a pinch of thyme, the grated peel of half a lemon, one raw egg, and flour enough to bind all together. Form into little balls the size of a hickory-nut; *sauté* them in a little hot butter. Or, It is very nice to add, instead of egg-balls, whole yolks of hard-boiled eggs, one for each plate.

The brains may be used for making croquettes (page 176), or as in receipt (page 151).

A simple Mock-turtle Soup.

Put four pig's feet, or calf's feet, and one pound of veal into four quarts of cold water, and let it simmer for five hours, reducing it to two quarts. Strain it, and let it remain overnight. The next day skim off the fat from the top, and remove the settlings from the bottom.

About half an hour before dinner put the soup on the fire, and season it with half a tea-spoonful of powdered thyme, a salt-spoonful of mace, a salt-spoonful of ground cloves. Simmer it for ten minutes. Now make a *roux* in a saucepan, viz.: put in one ounce of butter (size of a walnut), and, when it bubbles, sprinkle in one and a half ounces of flour (one table-spoonful). Stir it until the flour assumes a light-brown color; add the soup, and stir all together with the egg-whisk.

Make force-meat balls as follows: Chop some of the veal (used to make the soup), and about a quarter as much suet, very fine; season it with salt and pepper, and a few drops of lemon-juice; bind all together with some raw yolks of eggs and some cracker or bread crumbs; mold them into little balls about the size of a pigeon's egg, or smaller, if preferred. Fry them in boiling lard, or boil them two or three minutes in water. Cut up also some of the meat, or rather skin and cartilaginous substance, from the cold feet, which resembles turtle meat. Now put into the soup-tureen these meat-balls, pieces of calf's feet, and some yolks entire, or slices of hard-boiled eggs. Season the soup the last minute with a little lemon-juice and one or two table-spoonfuls of sherry.

For a small family, this will make soup enough for two dinners.

Gumbo Soup.

Ingredients: One large chicken; one and a half pints of green gumbo, or one pint of dried gumbo; three pints of water; pepper and salt.

Cut the chickens into joints, roll them in flour, and fry or *sauté* them in a little lard. Take out the pieces of chicken, and put in the sliced gumbo (either the green or the dried), and *sauté* that also until it is brown. Drain well the chickens and gumbo. There should be about a table-spoonful of brown fat left in the *sauté* pan; to this add a large table-spoonful of browned flour; then add the three pints of water, the chicken, cut into small pieces, and the gumbo. Simmer all together two hours. Strain through a colander. Serve boiled rice in another dish by the side of the soup-tureen. Having put a ladleful of the soup in the soup-plate, place a table-spoonful of rice in the centre.

Gumbo and Tomato Soup.

If canned gumbo and tomatoes mixed are used, merely add to them a pint or more of stock or strong beef broth. Bring them to the boiling-point, and season with pepper and salt.

If the fresh vegetables are used, boil the tomatoes and gumbo together for about half an hour, first frying the gumbo in a little hot lard. Many, however, boil the gumbo without frying.

Mullagatawny Soup (*an Indian soup*).

Cut up a chicken; put it into a soup-kettle, with a little sliced onion, carrot, celery, parsley, and three or four cloves. Cover it with four quarts of water. Add any pieces of veal, with the bones, you may have; of course, a knuckle of veal would be the proper thing. When the pieces of chicken are nearly done, take them out, and trim them neatly, to serve with the soup. Let the veal continue to simmer for three hours.

Now fry an onion, a small carrot, and a stick of celery sliced, in a little butter. When they are a light brown, throw in a table-spoonful of flour; stir it on the fire one or two minutes; then add a good tea-spoonful of curry powder, and the chicken and veal broth. Place this on the fire to simmer the usual way for an hour. Half an hour before dinner, strain the soup, skim off all the fat, return it to the fire with the pieces of chicken, and two or three table-spoonfuls of boiled rice. This will give time enough to cook the chickens thoroughly.

Oyster Soup.

To one quart, or twenty-five oysters, add a half pint of water. Put the oysters on the fire in the liquor. The moment it begins to simmer (not *boil*, for that would shrivel the oysters), pour it through a colander into a hot dish, leaving the oysters in the colander. Now put into the saucepan two ounces of butter (size of an egg); when it bubbles, sprinkle in a table-spoonful (one ounce) of sifted flour; let the *roux* cook a few moments, stirring it well with the egg-whisk; then add to it gradually the oyster-juice, and half a pint of good cream (which has been brought to a boil in another vessel); season carefully with Cayenne pepper and salt; skim well, then add the oysters. Do not let it boil, but serve immediately. An oyster soup is made with thickening; an oyster stew is made without it (see receipt).

Oyster crackers and pickles are often served with an oyster soup.

Clam Soup.

To extract the clams from the shells, wash them in cold water, and put them all into a large pot over the fire, containing half a cupful of boiling water; cover closely, and the steam will cause the clams to open; pour all into a colander over a pan, and extract the meat from the shells.

Put a quart of the clams with their liquor on the fire, with a pint of water; boil them about three minutes, during which time skim them well, then strain them. Beard them, and return the liquor to the fire, with the hard portions of the clams (keeping the soft portions aside in a warm place), half an onion (one ounce), a sprig of thyme, three or four sprigs of parsley, and one large blade of mace; cover it, and let it simmer for half an hour.

In the mean time make a *roux, i. e.,* put three ounces of butter (size of an egg) into a stew-pan, and when it bubbles sprinkle in two ounces of flour (one heaping table-spoonful); stir it on the fire until cooked, and then stir in gradually a pint of hot cream; add this to the clam liquor (strained), with a seasoning of salt and a little Cayenne pepper; also the soft clams, without chopping them. When well mixed, and thoroughly hot (without boiling), serve immediately.

BEAN SOUP.

Soak a quart of navy beans overnight. Then put them on the fire, with three quarts of water; three onions, fried or *sautéd* in a little butter; one little carrot; two potatoes, partly boiled in other water; a small cut of pork; a little red pepper, and salt. Let it all boil slowly for five or six hours. Pass it then through a colander or sieve. Return the pulp to the fire; season properly with salt and Cayenne pepper. Put into the tureen *croûtons*, or bread, cut in half-inch squares, and fried brown on all sides in a little butter or in boiling fat. Professor Blot adds broth, bacon, onions, celery, one or two cloves, and carrot to his bean soup. A French cook I once had added a little mustard to her bean soup, which made a pleasant change. Another cook adds cream at the last moment. Or,

A very good bean soup can be made from the remains of baked beans; the brown baked beans giving it a good color. Merely add water and a bit of onion; boil it to a pulp, and pass it through the colander.

If a little stock, or some bones or pieces of fresh meat are at hand, they add also to the flavor of bean soup.

BEAN AND TOMATO SOUP.

A pint of canned tomatoes, boiled, and passed through the sieve, with a quart of bean soup, makes a very pleasant change.

ONION SOUP (*Soupe à l'Ognon*).

A soup without meat, and delicious.

I was taught how to make this soup by a Frenchwoman; and it will be found a valuable addition to one's culinary knowledge. It is a good Friday soup.

Put into a saucepan butter size of a pigeon's egg. Clarified grease, or the cakes of fat saved from the top of stock, or soup (I always use the latter), answer about as well. When very hot, add two or three large onions, sliced thin; stir, and cook them well until they are red; then add a full half-tea-cupful of flour. Stir this also until it is red, watching it constantly, that it does not burn. Now pour in about a pint of boiling water, and add pepper and salt. Mix it well, and let it boil a minute; then pour it into the soup-kettle, and place it at the back of the range until almost ready to serve. Add then one and a half pints or a quart of boiling milk, and two or three well-mashed boiled potatoes. Add to the potatoes a little of the soup at first, then more, until they are smooth, and thin enough to put into the soup-kettle. Stir all well and smoothly together; taste, to see if the soup is properly seasoned with pepper and salt, as it requires plenty, especially of the latter. Let it simmer a few moments. Put pieces of toasted bread (a good way of using dry bread), cut in diamond shape, in the bottom of the tureen. Pour over the soup, and serve very hot. Or,

This soup might be made without potatoes, if more convenient, using more flour, and all milk instead of a little water. However, it is better with the potato addition; or it is much improved by adding stock instead of water; or, if one should chance to have a boiled chicken, the water in which it was boiled might be saved to make this soup.

VEGETABLE SOUP WITHOUT MEAT (*Purée aux Légumes*).

Cut up a large plateful of any and all kinds of vegetables one happens to have; for example, onions, carrots, potatoes (boiled in other water), beans (of any kind), parsnips, celery, pease, parsley, leeks, turnips, cauliflower, spinach, cabbage, etc., always having either potatoes or beans for a thickening. First put into a saucepan half a tea-cupful of butter (clarified suet or stock-pot fat is just as good). When it is very hot, put in first the cut-up onions. Stir them well, to prevent from burning. When they assume a fine red color, stir in a large table-spoonful of flour until it has the same color. Now stir in a pint of hot water, and some pepper and salt. Mind not to add pepper and salt at first, as the onions and flour would then more readily burn. Add, also, all the other vegetables. Let them simmer (adding more hot water when necessary) for two hours; then press them through a colander. Return them to the range in a soup-kettle, and let them simmer until the moment of serving.

CORN SOUP.

This is a very good soup, made with either fresh or canned corn. When it is fresh, cut the corn from the cob, and scrape off well all that sweetest part of the corn which remains on the cob. To a pint of corn add a quart of hot water. Boil it for an hour or longer; then press it through the colander. Put into the saucepan butter the size of a small egg, and when it bubbles sprinkle in a heaping table-spoonful of sifted flour, which cook a minute, stirring it well. Now add half of the corn pulp, and, when smoothly mixed, stir in the remainder of the corn: add Cayenne pepper, salt, a scant pint of boiling milk, and a cupful of cream.

This soup is very nice with no more addition, as it will have the pure taste of the corn; yet many add the yolks of two eggs just before serving, mixed with a little milk or cream, and not allowed to boil. Others add a table-spoonful of tomato catsup.

TOMATO SOUP, WITH RICE.

Cut half a small onion into rather coarse slices, and fry them in a little hot butter in a *sauté* pan. Add to them then a quart can, or ten or eleven large tomatoes cut in pieces, after having skinned them, and also two sprigs of parsley. Let it cook about ten minutes, when remove the pieces of onion and parsley. Pass the tomato through a sieve. Put into the stew-pan butter the size of a pigeon's egg, and when it bubbles sprinkle in a tea-spoonful of flour; when it has cooked a minute, stir in the tomato pulp: season with pepper and salt. It is an improvement to add a cupful or more of stock; however, if it is not at hand, it may be omitted.

Return the soup to the fire, and, when quite hot, add a cupful of fresh-boiled rice and half a tea-spoonful of soda.

TOMATO SOUP (*Purée aux Tomates*).—Mrs. Corbett.

Boil a dozen or a can of tomatoes until they are very thoroughly cooked, and press them through a sieve. To a quart of tomato pulp add a tea-spoonful of soda. Put into a saucepan butter the size of a pigeon's egg, and when it bubbles sprinkle and stir in a heaping tea-spoonful of flour. When it is cooked, stir into this a pint of hot milk, a little Cayenne pepper, salt, and a handful of cracker crumbs. When it boils, add the tomato pulp. Heat it well without boiling, and serve immediately.

The soda mixed with the tomatoes prevents the milk from curdling.

Sorrel Soup (*Soupe à la Bonne Femme*).

This is a most wholesome soup, which would be popular in America if it were better known. It is much used in France. Sorrel can be obtained, in season, at all the French markets in America.

For four quarts of soup, put into a saucepan a piece of butter the size of an egg, two or three sprigs of parsley, two or three leaves of lettuce, one onion, and a pint of sorrel (all finely chopped), a little nutmeg, pepper, and salt. Cover, and let them cook or sweat ten minutes; then add about two table-spoonfuls of flour. Mix well, and gradually add three quarts of boiling water (stock would be better). Make a *liaison, i. e.*, beat the yolks of four eggs (one egg to a quart of soup), and mix with them a cupful of cream or rich milk.

Add a little chevril (if you have it) to the soup; let it boil ten minutes; then stir in the eggs, or *liaison*, when the soup is quite ready.

Potato Soup (No. 1).

Fry seven or eight potatoes and a small sliced onion in a *sauté* pan in some butter or drippings—stock-pot fat is most excellent for this purpose. When they are a little colored, put them into two or three pints of hot water (stock would, of course, be better; yet hot water is oftenest used); add also a large heaping table-spoonful of chopped parsley. Let it boil until the potatoes are quite soft. Put all through the colander. Return the *purée* to the fire, and let it simmer two or three minutes. When just ready to serve, take the kettle off the fire; add plenty of salt and pepper, and the beaten yolks of two or three eggs. Do not let the soup boil when the eggs are in, as they would curdle.

Potato Soup (No. 2).

A very good soup for one which seems to have nothing in it.

Peel and cut up four rather large potatoes. When they are nearly done, pour off the water, and add one quart of hot water. Boil two hours, or until the potatoes are thoroughly dissolved in the water. Add fresh boiling water as it boils away. When done, run it through the colander, adding three-fourths of a cupful of hot cream, a large table-spoonful of finely cut parsley, salt, and pepper. Bring it to the boiling-point, and serve.

Purée of String-beans.

Make a strong stock as follows: Add to a knuckle of veal three quarts of water, a generous slice of salt pork, and two or three slices of onion. Let it simmer for five hours, then pour it through a sieve or colander into a jar. It is better to make this stock the day before it is served, as then every particle of fat may be easily scraped off the jelly.

Ten minutes before dinner, put into a saucepan two ounces of butter, and when it bubbles sprinkle in four ounces of flour (two heaping table-spoonfuls); let it cook without taking color; then add a cupful of hot cream, a pint of the heated stock, and about a pint of green string-bean pulp, *i. e.*, either fresh or canned string-beans boiled tender with a little pork, then pressed through a colander, and freed from juice. After mixing all together, do not let the soup boil, or it will curdle and spoil. Stir it constantly while it is on the fire.

Just before it is sent to table, sprinkle over the top a handful of little fried fritter-beans. They are made by dropping *drops* of fritter batter into boiling lard. They will resemble navy-beans, and give a very pleasant flavor and appearance to the soup.

If this pretty addition be considered too much trouble, little dice of fried bread (*croûtons*) may be added instead. The soup should be rather thick, and served quite hot.

Bisque of Lobsters.

This soup is made exactly like the *purée* of string-beans, with the veal stock and thickened cream, except that, in place of the string-bean pulp, the soup is now flavored and colored with the coral of lobster, dried in the oven, and pounded fine. This gives it a beautiful pink color. Little dice of the boiled lobster are then to be added. The lobster-dice may or may not be marinated before they are added to the soup, *i. e.*, sprinkled with a mixture of one table-spoonful of oil, three table-spoonfuls of vinegar, pepper, and salt, and left for two or three hours in the marinade. Season the soup with pepper and salt.

FISH.

If a fish is not perfectly fresh, perfectly cleaned, and thoroughly cooked, it is not eatable. It should be cleaned or drawn as soon as it comes from market, then put on the ice until the time of cooking. It should not be soaked, for it impairs the flavor, unless it is frozen, when it should be put into ice-cold water to thaw; or unless it is a salted fish, when it may be soaked overnight.

The greatest merit of a fish is freshness. The secret of the excellence of the fish at the Saratoga Lake House, where they have famous trout dinners, is that, as they are raised on the premises, they go almost immediately from the pond to the fish-kettle. One is to be pitied who has not tasted fish at the sea-shore, where fishermen come in just before dinner, with baskets filled with blue-fish, flounders, etc., fresh from the water.

A long, oval fish-kettle (page 52) is very convenient for frying or boiling fish. It has a strainer to fit, in which the fish is placed, enabling it to be taken from the kettle without breaking. A fish is sufficiently cooked when the meat separates easily from the bones. When the fish is quite done, it should be left no longer in the kettle; it will lose its flavor.

It makes a pleasant change to cook fish *"au gratin."* It is a simple operation, but little attempted in America. I would recommend this mode of cooking for eels, or the Western white-fish.

A fish is most delicious fried in olive-oil. A friend told me he purchased olive-oil by the keg, for cooking purposes. It is, of course, expensive, and lard or beef drippings answer very well. I would recommend, also, frying fish by *immersion*.

If a fish is to be served whole, do not cut off the head and tail. It also presents a better appearance to stand the fish on its belly rather than lay it on its side.

To Boil Fish.

All fish but salmon (which is put into warm water to preserve its color) should be placed in salted *cold* water, with a little vinegar or lemon-juice in it, to boil. It should then boil *very, very* gently, or the outside will break before the inside is done. It requires a little experience to know exactly how long to boil a fish. It must never be underdone; yet it must be taken from the water as soon as it is thoroughly done, or it will become insipid, watery, and colorless. It will require about eight minutes to the pound for large, thick fish, and about five minutes to the pound for thin fish, after the water begins to simmer, using only enough water to cover it. When done, drain it well before the fire. The fresh-water, or any kind of fish which have no decided flavor, are much better boiled *au court bouillon,* or with onions and carrots (sliced), parsley, two or three cloves, pepper, salt, vinegar, or wine—any or all of these added to the water. The sea-fish, or such as have a flavor *prononcé,* can be boiled in simple salted and acidulated water.

If you have no fish-kettle, and wish to boil a fish, arrange it in a circle on a plate, with an old napkin around it: when it is done, it can be carefully lifted from the kettle by the cloth, so that it will not be broken. When cuts of fish are boiled, you allow the water to just come to a boil; then remove the kettle to the back of the range, so that it will only simmer.

Always serve a sauce with a boiled fish, such as drawn butter, egg, caper, pickle, shrimp, oyster, *Hollandaise,* or piquante sauce.

To Boil Au Court Bouillon.

Among professional cooks, a favorite way of boiling a fish is in water saturated with vegetables, called *court bouillon*; consequently, a fish cooked in this manner would be called, for instance, "Pike, *au court bouillon.*" It is rather a pity this way of cooking has a French name; however, if one is not unduly scared at that, one can see how simple it is.

Dubois's Receipt.—Mince a carrot, an onion, and a small piece of celery; fry them in a little butter, in a stew-pan; add some parsley, some peppercorns, and three or four cloves. Now pour on two quarts of hot water and a pint of vinegar. Let it boil a quarter of an hour; skim it, salt it, and use it for boiling the fish.

It is improved by using white or red wine instead of vinegar; only use then three parts of wine to one of water. These stocks are easily preserved, and may be used several times.

To boil the fish: Rub the fish with lemon-juice and salt, put it in a kettle, and cover it with *court bouillon.* Let it only simmer, not boil hard, until thoroughly done. Serve the fish on a napkin, surrounded with parsley. Serve a caper, pickle, or any kind of fish sauce, in a sauce-boat.

To Fry Fish.

By frying fish I mean that it is to be *immersed* in hot lard, beef drippings, or olive-oil. Let there be a little more fat than will cover the fish; otherwise it is liable to stick to the bottom and burn. Do not put in the fish until the fat is tested, and found to be quite hot. If the fat were not hot enough, the fish would absorb some of it, making it greasy and unwholesome. If it is hot enough, the fish will absorb nothing at all.

To prepare fish for frying, dredge them first with flour; then brush them with beaten egg, and roll them in fine or sifted bread, or cracker crumbs. When they are browned on one side, turn them over in the hot fat. When done, let them drain quite dry.

Cutlets of any large fish are particularly nice egged and bread-crumbed, fried, and served with tomato sauce or slices of lemon.

Fish Fried in Batter.

Cut almost any kind of fish in fillets or pieces one-fourth of an inch thick, and one or two inches square; only be careful to have them all of the same shape and size. Sprinkle them with pepper and salt, and roll each one in batter (No. 2, page 98). Fry them in boiling lard. Arrange them tastefully in a circle, one overlapping the other. Garnish with fresh or fried parsley. Potatoes *à la Parisienne* may be piled in the centre, and *sauce Tartare*

To Broil Fish.

The same rule applies to broiling fish as to every thing else. If the fish is small, it requires a clear, hot fire. If the fish is large, the fire must be moderate; otherwise the outside of the fish would be burned before the inside is cooked. Many rub the fish over with olive-oil; others split a large fish; still others broil it whole, and cut notches at equal distances across its sides. When you wish to turn the fish, separate carefully with a knife any part of it which sticks to the gridiron; then, holding a platter over the fish with one hand, turn the gridiron over with the other, leaving the fish on the platter: it will now be a more easy matter to turn it without breaking. As soon as the fish is done, sprinkle over pepper and salt, and spread butter all over it with a knife. Set it in the oven a moment, so that the butter may soak in the fish. This is the most common way of seasoning it. It is almost as easy to first sprinkle pepper and salt, then a few drops of lemon-juice, over the fish; then a table-spoonful of parsley, chopped fine; then some melted butter over all. Put it a moment in the oven to soak. They call this a *maître-d'hôtel* sauce. Quite simple, is it not? It is especially nice for a broiled shad.

To Bake Fish.

When cleaning the fish, do not cut off the head and tail. Stuff it. Two or three receipts are given for the stuffing. Sew it, or confine the stuffing by winding the cord several times around the fish. Lay several pieces of pork, cut in strings, across the top; sprinkle over water, pepper, salt, and bread-crumbs; put some hot water into the pan; bake in a hot oven, *basting very often*. When done (the top should be nicely browned), serve a sauce with it. The best fishes to bake are white-fish, blue-fish, shad, etc. If not basted very often, a baked fish will be very dry. For this reason, an ordinary cook should never bake a fish. I believe, however, they never cook them in any other way.

STUFFINGS FOR FISH.

Bread Stuffing.

Soak half a pound of bread-crumbs in water; when the bread is soft, press out all the water. Fry two table-spoonfuls of minced onion in some butter; add the bread, some chopped parsley, a table-spoonful of chopped suet, and pepper and salt. Let it cook a moment; take it off the fire, and add an egg.

Meat Stuffing.

This stuffing is best made with veal, and almost an equal quantity of bacon chopped fine. Put in a quarter of its volume of white softened bread-crumbs, pressed out well; add a little chopped onion, parsley, or mushrooms; season highly.

If the fish should be baked with wine, this dressing can be used, viz.:

Soak about three slices of bread. When the water is well pressed out, season it with salt, a little cayenne, a little mace, and moisten it with port-wine or sherry; add the juice and the grated rind of half a lemon.

To Bake a Fish with Wine (*Mrs. Samuel Treat*).

Stuff a fish with the following dressing. Soak some bread in water, squeeze it dry, and add an egg well beaten. Season it with pepper, salt, and a little parsley or thyme; grease the baking-pan (one just the right size for holding the fish) with butter; season the fish on top, and put it into the pan with about two cups of boiling water; baste it well, adding more boiling water when necessary. About twenty minutes before serving, pour over it a cup of sour wine, and a small piece of butter (Mrs. Treat adds also two or three table-spoonfuls of Worcestershire sauce mixed with the wine—of course, this may be left out if more convenient); put half a lemon, sliced, into the gravy; baste the fish again well. When it is thoroughly baked, remove it from the pan; garnish the top with the slices of lemon; finish the sauce in the baking-dish by adding a little butter rubbed to a paste in some flour; strain, skim, and serve it in a sauce-boat.

To Stew Fish, or Fish en Matelote.

Cut the fish transversely into pieces about an inch or an inch and a half long; sprinkle salt on them, and let them remain while you boil two or three onions (sliced) in a very little water; pour off this water when the onions are cooked, and add to them pepper, about a tea-cupful of hot water, and a tea-cupful of wine if it is claret or white wine, and two or three table-spoonfuls if it is sherry or port: now add the fish. When it begins to simmer, throw in some little balls of butter which have been rolled in flour. When the fish is thoroughly cooked, serve it very hot. This is a very good manner of cooking any fresh-water fish.

Fish is much better stewed with some wine. Of course, it is quite possible to stew fish without it, in which case add a little parsley.

To Cook Fish au Gratin.

This is a favorite manner with the French of cooking fish. The fish is served in the same dish in which it is cooked. It is called a *gratin* dish—generally an oval silver-plated platter, or it may be of block-tin. A fish *au gratin* is rather expensive, on account of the mushrooms; however, the French canned mushrooms (*champignons*) are almost as good as fresh ones, and are much cheaper.

Receipt.—First put into a saucepan butter size of an egg, then a handful of shallots, or one large onion minced fine; let it cook ten minutes, when mix in half a cupful of flour; then mince three-fourths of a cupful of mushrooms. Add a tea-cupful of hot water (or better, stock) to the saucepan, then a glass of white or red wine, salt, and pepper. After mixing them well, add the minced mushrooms and a little minced parsley. Skin the fish, cut off the head and tail, split it in two, laying bare the middle bone; slip the knife under the bone, removing it smoothly. Now cut the fish in pieces about an inch long. Moisten the *gratin* dish with butter, arrange the cuts of fish tastefully on it, pour over the sauce, then sprinkle the whole with bread-crumbs which have been dried and grated. Put little pieces of butter over all, and bake. The dish may be garnished with little diamonds of fried or toasted and buttered bread around the edge. Or,

This is a pretty dish *au gratin*: Put mashed potatoes (which must be still hot when arranged) in a circle on the outside of the *gratin* dish, then a row of the pieces of fish (which have been cooked as just described) around the middle of the dish, or just inside the potatoes. Put some mashed potatoes also in the middle of the dish. Garnish here and there with mushrooms. Pour the sauce just described and bread-crumbs over the fish, and bake five or ten minutes.

Fish à la Crème (*Mrs. Audenreid*).

Boil a fish weighing four pounds in salted water. When done, remove the skin, and flake it, leaving out the bones. Boil one quart of rich milk. Mix butter size of a small egg with three table-spoonfuls of flour, and stir it smoothly in the milk, adding also two or three sprigs of parsley and half an onion chopped fine, a little Cayenne pepper, and salt. Stir it over the fire until it has thickened.

Butter a *gratin* dish. Put in first a layer of fish, then of dressing, and continue in alternation until all the fish is used, with dressing on top. Sprinkle sifted bread-crumbs over the top. Bake half an hour. Garnish with parsley and slices of hard-boiled egg.

As the rules for boiling, broiling, frying, cooking *au gratin*, and stewing are the same for nearly all kinds of fish, I will not repeat the receipts for each particular one. I will only suggest the best manner for cooking certain kinds, and will add certain receipts not under the general rule:

SALMON

is undoubtedly best boiled. The only exception to the rule of boiling fish is in the case of salmon, which must be put in hot instead of cold water, to preserve its color. A favorite way of boiling a whole salmon is in the form of a letter S, as in plate. It is done as follows: Thread a trussing-needle with some twine; tie the end of the string around the head, fastening it tight; then pass the needle through the centre part of the body, draw the string tight, and fasten it around the tail. The fish will assume the desired form.

For parties or evening companies, salmon boiled in this form (middle cuts are also used), served cold, with a *Mayonnaise* sauce poured over, is a favorite dish. It is then generally mounted in style, on an oval or square block pedestal, three or four inches high, made of bread (two or three days old), called a *croustade*, carved in any form with a sharp knife. It is then fried a light-brown in boiling lard. Oftener these *croustades* are made of wood, which are covered with white paper, and brushed over with a little half-set aspic jelly. The salmon is then decorated with squares of aspic jelly. A decoration of quartered hard-boiled eggs or of cold cauliflower-blossoms is very pretty, and is palatable also with the *Mayonnaise* sauce. The best sauces for a boiled salmon served hot are the *sauce Hollandaise,* lobster, shrimp, or oyster sauces—the *sauce Hollandaise* being the favorite.

If lobster sauce is used, the coral of the lobster is dried, and sprinkled over the fish, reserving some with which to color the sauce, as in receipt for lobster sauce

If shrimp sauce is used, some whole shrimps should be saved for decorating the dish.

In decorating salmon, as well as any other kind of fish, potatoes cut in little balls, and placed like little piles of cannon-balls around the dish, are pretty. The potatoes should be simply boiled in salted water. An alternate pile of button mushrooms are pretty, and good also. Parsley or any pretty leaves around a dish always give a fresh and tasteful appearance. Or,

An exceedingly pretty garnish for a large fish is one of smelts (in rings, fried in boiling lard. In this case, add slices of lemon. Still another pretty garnish is of fried oysters or fried parsley, or both.

It is quite appropriate to serve a middle cut of salmon at a dinner: 1st, because it is the best cut; 2d, because it is easier and cheaper to serve; and, 3d, because one never cares to supply more than is necessary. This cut is better slowly boiled, also, in the acidulated salted water.

To Broil Salmon.

Take two slices of salmon cut from the middle of the fish, sprinkle over a little lemon-juice, Cayenne pepper, salt, and salad-oil. Let it then remain for half an hour. Rub the gridiron well with beef-suet or pork. As it is a nice matter to broil salmon without burning, it would be well to wrap it in buttered or oiled paper just before broiling. Serve a *maître-d'hôtel*, pickle, caper, anchovy, or a horse-radish sauce.

Salmon Cutlets.

Remove the skin and bone from some slices of salmon one-third of an inch thick; trim them into cutlet shape; sprinkle on pepper, salt, and flour, and dip them into beaten eggs mixed with a little chopped parsley or onion; then bread-crumb them. Fry them in boiling lard. This is the better way, or they may be fried or *sautéd* in butter in a *sauté* pan. Arrange the pieces one over the other in a circle. Pour a pickle, or *Tartare* sauce, in the centre.

Slices of Salmon Boiled.

If a family is small, and it should not be advisable to buy a large middle cut of salmon, it would be preferable to buy, for instance, two slices. Boil them very slowly in acidulated salted water, or in the *court bouillon* with wine. Serve them with parsley between, and a napkin underneath. Serve a *sauce Hollandaise* in the sauce-boat.

Canned Salmon.

The California canned salmon is undoubtedly one of the greatest successes in canning. By keeping a few cans in the house, one is always ready in any emergency to produce a fine dish of salmon in a few minutes. It is particularly nice for a breakfast-dish, heated, seasoned with pepper and salt, placed on thin slices of buttered toast, with a cream dressing poured over all, *i. e.*, milk thickened on the fire, by stirring it into a *roux* of butter and flour, and seasoned with pepper, salt, and a few pieces of fresh butter just before serving. For dinner it is excellent served with any of the fish sauces. Salmon is also nice served in shells, as for trout

SHAD.

This delicious fish is undoubtedly best broiled, with a *maître-d'hôtel* sauce; but it is good also cut in slices, and *sautéd*.

TROUT.

If large, they may be broiled, boiled, or baked. If boiled or broiled, serve the *sauce Hollandaise* with them. Professional cooks generally boil it in the *court bouillon*. Smaller trout are better egged, rolled in salted corn-meal, and thrown into boiling lard.

The trout is a very nice fish for an *au gratin*, or stewed, called then *en matelote*.

Trout in Cases or in Shells (*en Coquilles*).

Parboil little trout; cut the fish into pieces about an inch long, or into dice; place them in paper cases (which have been buttered or oiled, and placed in the oven a few moments to harden the paper so as to enable it to hold the sauce). After partly filling the cases with the pieces of fish, pour over them some fine herb sauce and sprinkle over bread-crumbs; put them into the oven twenty minutes before dinner to bake.

If shells are used, little plated-silver ones (scallop shells) are preferable. In that case, it would be better to fry the fish (seasoned with pepper, salt, and a little lemon-juice) in a *sauté* pan; cut them in dice afterward, and put them in the shells; pour over a fine herb or a Bechamel sauce; strew the top with grated bread-crumbs; place them a few moments in the oven to brown the tops, and serve.

COD-FISH.

Fresh cod-fish is better boiled. The fish is so large that it is generally boiled in slices. After it is well salted, horse-radish and vinegar in the boiling water will improve the fish. Oyster-sauce is the favorite sauce for a boiled cod-fish. Capers might be mixed with the oyster-sauce. Some serve the fish with the sauce poured over it. Any of the fish sauces may be served with fresh cod-fish. These slices may also be broiled and served with a *maître-d'hôtel* sauce, or they may be egged and bread-crumbed, and fried in boiling lard.

CRIMPED COD-FISH (*Rudmanii*).

Soak two slices of cod-fish one inch thick for two hours in ice-water; put them into the stew-pan, and, pouring over enough salted boiling water to cover them, let them *simmer* for about ten minutes; place them neatly on a platter on a folded napkin, garnish with parsley, and pour into the two cavities a *Tartare* or a pickle sauce.

SALT COD-FISH.

Soak this in water overnight; parboil it, changing the water once or twice; separate the flakes. Serve them on thin slices of toast, with an egg sauce poured over. Or,

Mince it when boiled in very little water, which should be changed once; thicken it with butter and flour mixed; cook about two minutes, then break in several eggs. When the eggs are cooked and mixed with the fish, pour all on thin slices of buttered toast.

COD-FISH BALLS.

Cut the cod-fish in pieces; soak them about an hour in lukewarm water, when the bones and skin may be easily removed; pull the fish then into fine shreds, and put it on the stove in some cold water. As soon as it begins to boil, change the water, and repeat this process a second time. It is not proper to boil it, as it renders it tough. As soon as the fish is ready, some potatoes must be cooked at the same time, *i. e.*, boiled tender, and well-mashed while still hot, with a little butter added. Mix half as much cod-fish as potatoes while both are *still hot*. Form them into little balls or thick flat cakes. Fry them in a little hot butter in a *sauté* pan, or immerse them in boiling-hot lard. It makes all the difference in the flavor of the balls if the fish and potatoes are mixed while both are *hot*. Of course, they are better fried at once, but may be made the night before serving (at breakfast), if they are only properly *mixed*.

Fish Chowder.

Cut three pounds of any kind of fresh fish (cod-fish is especially good), one and a half pounds of potatoes, and one large onion (three ounces) into slices; also, half a pound of salt pork into half-inch squares or dice.

Put the pork and onions into a saucepan, and fry them a light brown; then add a cupful of claret; and when it boils take it from the fire.

Butter a large stew-pan, and put in first a layer of potatoes, then a layer of fish, then a sprinkle of onions and pork (strained from the claret), pepper and salt, and continue these alternations until it is all in, having the potatoes on top. Now pour the claret over the top, and barely cover the whole with boiling water. Cover closely, and let it simmer for fifteen minutes without disturbing it.

In the mean time, bring a pint of milk (or, better, cream) to a boil, take it from the fire, and cut into it three ounces of butter, and break in three ship-crackers. Arrange the slices of fish and potatoes in the shape of a dome in the centre of a hot platter. Place the softened crackers (skimmed from the milk) over the top, and pour over the milk. Serve very hot.

Small Pan-fish (*Perch, Sun-fish, etc.*).

They are generally preferred peppered, salted, then rolled in salted corn-meal, and fried either in a *sauté* pan with a little lard and some slices of pork, or in boiling lard. They make also a good stew *en matelote*, or a good *au gratin*. Their chief excellence consists in their being perfectly fresh, and served hot.

MACKEREL

should be broiled, and served *à la maître-d'hôtel*.

SMELTS

are good salted, peppered, and rolled in salted corn-meal or flour, and fried in boiling-hot lard, but better egged and bread-crumbed before frying. They should be served *immediately,* or they will lose their crispness and flavor. When served as a garnish for a large fish, they should be fried in the shape of rings. This is easily done by putting the tail of the fish into its mouth, and holding it with a pin. After it is fried, the pin is withdrawn, as the fried fish will hold its shape. Place these rings around the fish, with an additional garnish of parsley and lemon slices; or the rings may be served alone in a circle around the side of a platter, with a tomato or a *Tartare* sauce in the centre.

There can be no prettier manner of serving them alone than one often seen in Paris. They are fried in the usual manner; then a little silver or silver-plated skewer four inches long is drawn through two or three of the smelts, running it carefully through the eyes. One skewerful, with a slice of lemon on top, is served for each person at table. If the silver-plated skewers are too extravagant, little ones of polished wire will answer.

Fried Slices of Fish, with Tomato Sauce (*Fish à l'Orlay*).

Bone and skin the fish, and cut it into even slices; or if a flounder or any flat fish is used, begin at the tail, and, keeping the knife close to the bone, separate each side of the fish neatly from it; then cut each side in two, lengthwise, leaving the fish in four long pieces. Remove the skin carefully. After having sprinkled pepper and salt over them, roll each piece first in sifted cracker or bread crumbs, then in half a cupful of milk mixed with an egg, and then in the crumbs again. They are better fried in a *sauté* pan in a little hot butter; yet they may be *sautéd* in a little hot lard, with some neat slices of pork, or fried in boiling lard.

To Fry Eels.

Skin them, cut them into four-inch lengths, season them with salt and pepper, roll them in flour or salted corn-meal, and fry them in boiling lard. Some parboil eels and bull-heads, saying it removes a muddy taste. I do not think it is necessary. Fried eels are generally served with a tomato, a pickle, or a *Tartare* sauce.

Eels Stewed (*London Cooking-school*).

Put three-quarters of a cupful of butter into a stew-pan; when hot, add four small onions minced fine, which cook to a light-brown color; add then a table-spoonful of flour; when well mixed and cooked, add two cupfuls of stock, a wine-glassful of port-wine, and two bay leaves (the bay leaves may be omitted). Now put in the eels (two small ones or one large one), cut into pieces one inch long. Cover tightly.

They will be ready to send to the table in about fifteen minutes, served on a hot platter, with a circle around them of toasted or fried slices of bread (*croûtons*), cut diamond-shaped.

SHELL-FISH.

OYSTERS.

Raw Oysters.

Drain them well in a colander, marinate them, *i. e.*, sprinkle over plenty of pepper and salt, and let them remain in a cold place for at least half an hour before serving. This makes a great difference in their flavor. They may be served in the half-shell with quarters or halves of lemons in the same dish. I think a prettier arrangement is to serve them in a block of ice. Select a ten-pound block; melt with a hot flat-iron a symmetrical-shaped cavity in the top to hold the oysters; chip also from the sides at the base, so that the ice-block may stand in a large platter on the napkin. When the oysters are well salted and peppered, place them in the ice, and let them remain in some place where the ice will not melt until the time of serving. The salt will help to make the oysters very cold. The ice may be decorated with leaves or smilax vines, and a row of lemon quarters or halves may be placed around the platter at the base of the ice. It has an especially pretty effect served on a table by gas-light. The English often serve little thin squares of buttered brown bread (like Boston brown bread) with oysters.

Fried Oysters.

Drain the oysters in the colander; sprinkle over pepper and salt, which mix well with them, and put them in a cold place for fifteen or twenty minutes before cooking. This is marinating them. When ready to cook, roll each one first in sifted cracker-crumbs, then in beaten egg mixed with a little milk and seasoned with pepper and salt, then in the cracker-crumbs again. You will please remember the routine: *first*, the crumbs before the egg, as the egg will not adhere well to the oyster without the crumbs; now throw them into boiling-hot lard (as you would fry doughnuts), first testing to see if it is hot enough. As soon as they assume a light-brown color they should be drained, and served immediately on a hot platter.

Oysters should not be fried until the persons at table are ready to eat them, as it takes only a few moments to fry them, and they are not good unless very hot.

The platter of oysters may be garnished with a table-spoonful of chopped pickles or chowchow placed at the four opposite sides; or the oysters may be served as a border around cold slaw (see receipt, page 224), when they are an especially nice course for dinner; or they may be served with celery, either plain or in salad. As the platter for the fried oysters is hot, the celery salad or cold slaw might be piled on a folded napkin in the centre.

Scalloped Oysters in Shells.

They may be served cooked in their shells, or in silver scallop shells, when they present a better appearance than when cooked and served all in one dish.

If cooked in an oyster or clam shell, one large, or two or three little oysters are placed in it, with a few drops of the oyster liquor. It is sprinkled with pepper and salt, and cracker or bread crumbs. Little pieces of butter are placed over the top. When all are ready, they are put into the oven. When they are plump and hot, they are done. Brown the tops with a salamander, or with a red-hot kitchen shovel.

If they are cooked in the silver scallop shells, which are larger, several oysters are served in the one shell; one or two are put in, peppered, salted, strewed with cracker-crumbs and small pieces of butter; then more layers, until the shell is full, or until enough are used for one person. Moisten them with the oyster-juice, and strew little pieces of butter over the top. They are merely kept in the oven until they are thoroughly hot, then browned with a salamander. Serve one shell for each person at table, placed on a small plate. The oysters may be bearded or not.

Scalloped Oysters.

Ingredients: Three dozen oysters, a large tea-cupful of bread or cracker crumbs, two ounces of fresh butter, pepper and salt, half a tea-cupful of oyster-juice.

Make layers of these ingredients, as described in the last article, in the top of a chafing-dish, or in any kind of pudding or *gratin* dish; bake in a quick oven about fifteen minutes; brown with a salamander.

Oyster Stew.

Put a quart of oysters on the fire in their own liquor. The moment they *begin* to boil, skim them out, and add to the liquor a half-pint of hot cream, salt, and Cayenne pepper to taste. Skim it well, take it off the fire, add to the oysters an ounce and a half of butter broken into small pieces. Serve immediately.

Oyster or Clam Fritters.

Oysters served on buttered toast for breakfast, or in *vols-au-vent*, silver scallop-shells, or in paper boxes, are very nice made after the receipts on page 241. They or the fricasseed oysters may be served in either of the above ways.

Fricassee of Oysters (*Oysters à la Boulette*).

Put one quart, or twenty-five, oysters on the fire in their own liquor. The moment it begins to boil, turn it into a hot dish through a colander, leaving the oysters in the colander. Put into the saucepan two ounces of butter (size of an egg), and when it bubbles sprinkle in one ounce (a table-spoonful) of sifted flour; let it cook a minute without taking color, stirring it well with a wire egg-whisk; then add, mixing well, a cupful of the oyster liquor. Take it from the fire and mix in the yolks of two eggs, a little salt, a very little Cayenne pepper, one tea-spoonful of lemon-juice, and one grating of nutmeg. Beat it well; then return it to the fire to set the eggs, without allowing it to boil. Put in the oysters.

These oysters may be served on thin slices of toast for breakfast or tea, or in papers (*en papillote*), or as a filling for patties for dinner.

To Roast Canned Oysters.

Drain them. Put them in a spider which is very hot; turn them in a moment, so that they may cook on both sides. It only takes a few seconds to cook them. Put them on a hot plate in which there are pepper, salt, and a little hot melted butter. They should be served immediately. They have the flavor of the oyster roasted in the shell.

Some cook them in this manner at table on a chafing-dish by means of the spirit-lamp.

Spiced Oysters (*Miss Lestlie*).

Ingredients: Two hundred oysters, one pint of vinegar, a nutmeg grated, eight blades of whole mace, three dozen whole cloves, one tea-spoonful of salt, two tea-spoonfuls of whole allspice, and as much Cayenne pepper as will lie on the point of a knife.

Put the oysters with their liquor into a large earthen vessel; add to them the vinegar and all the other ingredients. Stir all well together and set them over a slow fire, keeping them covered. Stir them to the bottom several times. As soon as they are well scalded, they are done. To be eaten cold.

CLAMS.

Clams Cooked with Cream (*Mrs. Audenreid*).

Chop fifty small clams not too fine, and season them with pepper and salt. Put into a stew-pan butter the size of an egg, and when it bubbles sprinkle in a tea-spoonful of flour, which cook a few moments; stir gradually into it the clam liquor, then the clams, which stew about two or three minutes; then add a cupful of boiling cream, and serve immediately. The clams may or may not be bearded.

Clam Chowder.

Put fifty clams on the fire in their own liquor, with a little salt. When they have boiled about three minutes, strain them, and return the liquor to the fire. Chop a medium-sized onion (two ounces) into small pieces, and cut six ounces of pork into dice. Fry both a light color in two ounces (size of an egg) of butter; then stir in three ounces of flour (two table-spoonfuls). When thoroughly cooked, add the clam liquor, half a pint of good stock or milk, the same quantity of cream, a salt-spoonful of mace, a salt-spoonful of thyme, salt to taste, and eight ounces of potatoes cut into dice. When these are cooked, and the chowder is about to be sent to table, add the clams cut in dice, and four ounces of ship-bread or crackers broken in pieces.

Tunison Clam Chowder.

Ingredients: Two hundred soft clams, one large onion, twenty large crackers, can of tomatoes, parsley (chopped fine), half a pound of butter, one large tea-spoonful of sweet marjoram, thyme, sage, savory, half a tea-spoonful of ground cloves, and half a tea-spoonful of curry.

Boil well; then add half a pint of milk and half a pint of sherry wine.

CRABS AND LOBSTERS.

Soft-shell Crabs.

Dry them; sprinkle them with pepper and salt; roll them, first in flour, then in egg (half a cupful of milk mixed in one egg), then in cracker-dust, and fry them in boiling lard.

Deviled Crab.

When the crabs are boiled, take out the meat and cut it into small pieces (dice); clean well the shells.

To six ounces of crab meat, mix two ounces of bread-crumbs, two hard-boiled eggs chopped, the juice of half a lemon, Cayenne pepper and salt. Mix all with cream or cream sauce, or, what is still better, a Bechamel sauce Fill the shells with the mixture, smooth the tops, sprinkle over sifted bread-crumbs, and color it in a quick oven.

Deviled Lobster

is made in the same way as deviled crab, merely substituting the lobster for the crab, and adding a grating of nutmeg to the seasoning. In boiling lobsters and crabs, they are sufficiently cooked when they assume a bright-red color. Too much boiling renders them tough.

Lobster Chops.

Cut half a pound of the flesh of a boiled lobster into small dice. Put two ounces of butter into a stew-pan, and when it bubbles sprinkle in two ounces of flour (one table-spoonful). Cook it; then pour in a cupful of boiling cream and the lobster dice. Stir it until it is scalding hot; then take it from the fire, and, when slightly cooled, stir in the beaten yolks of three eggs, a grating of nutmeg, a little Cayenne pepper, and salt to taste. Return the mixture to the fire, and stir it long enough to well set the eggs.

Butter a platter, on which spread the lobster mixture half an inch deep. When cold, form it into the shape of chops, pointed at one end; bread-crumb, egg, and crumb them again, and fry them in boiling lard. Stick a claw into the end of each lobster chop after it is cooked.

Place the chops in a circle, overlapping each other, on a napkin. Decorate the dish by putting the tail of the lobster in the centre, and its head, with the long horns, on the tail. Around the outside of the circle of chops arrange the legs, cut an inch each side of the middle joints, so that they will form two equal sides of a triangle.

A Good Way to Prepare a Lobster.

Put into a saucepan butter the size of a small egg, and a tea-spoonful of minced onion. When it has cooked, sprinkle in a tea-spoonful of flour, which cook also; then stir in one cupful of the water in which the lobster was boiled, one cupful of milk, one cupful of strong veal or beef stock, pepper, and salt: add the meat of the boiled lobster, and when quite hot pour all in the centre of a hot platter. Decorate the dish with the lobster's head in the centre, fried-bread diamonds (*croûtons*) around the outside; or in any prettier way you choose, with the abundant resources of lobster legs and trimmings.

FROGS.

Frogs are such a delicacy that it is a pity not to prepare them with care.

The hind legs only are used. They may be made into a broth the same as chicken broth, and are considered a very advantageous diet for those suffering with pulmonary affections.

Frogs Fried.

Put them in salted boiling water, with a little lemon-juice, and boil them three minutes; wipe them; dip them first in cracker-dust, then in eggs (half a cupful of milk mixed in two eggs and seasoned with pepper and salt), then again in cracker-crumbs. When they are all breaded, clean off the bone at the end with a dry cloth. Put them in a wire basket and dip them in boiling lard, to fry. Put a little paper (see page 61) on the end of each bone; place them on a hot platter, in the form of a circle, one overlapping the other, with French pease in the centre. Serve immediately, while they are still crisp and hot.

SAUCES.

The French say the English only know how to make one kind of sauce, and a poor one at that. Notwithstanding the French understand the sauce question, it is very convenient to make the drawn butter, and, by adding different flavorings, make just so many kinds of sauce. For instance, by adding capers, shrimps, chopped pickles, anchovy paste, chopped boiled eggs, lobster, oysters, parsley, cauliflower, etc., one has caper, shrimp, pickle, anchovy, egg, and the other sauces. The drawn-butter sauce is simple, yet few make it properly, managing generally to have it insipid, and with flour uncooked. If a housekeeper has any pride about having a good table, she will be amply repaid for learning some of the French sauces, which are, at last, simple enough. We are often frightened to see many items in a receipt; we shake our heads dubiously at the trouble and extravagance of one receipt mentioning thyme, nutmeg, bay-leaf, mace, shallot, capers, pepper-corns, parsley, and, last of all the horrors, stock. As far as the herbs are concerned, an investment of twenty-five cents will purchase enough mace, thyme, bay-leaves, and pepper-corns for a year's supply of abundant sauces, to say nothing of their uses for braising, *blanquettes*, etc. Five cents' worth of shallots should last a long time; they are sold in all city markets, being only young forced onions. Capers would be extravagant if a bottleful, costing sixty cents, would not last a year in a small-sized family. I have already said enough about stock to show that one must be very incompetent if a little of it can not be at hand, made of trimmings and cheap pieces of meat and bones.

The use of mushrooms and truffles, which are comparatively cheap in France, can not be extensively introduced here. A little tin can, holding about a gill of tasteless truffles, costs three or four dollars: however, mushrooms are much less expensive, and infinitely better. A can of mushrooms costs forty cents, and is sufficient for several sauces and *entrées*.

Some persons raise mushrooms in their cellars. A small, rich bed in a dark place where the soil will not freeze, planted with mushroom spawn, will yield enough mushrooms for the family, and the neighbors besides, with very little trouble and expense.

The French white sauces differ from the English white sauce, as they are made with strong white stock, prepared with veal, or chickens, or both, and some vegetables for a basis. If one would learn to make the *sauce Bechamel*, it will be found an easy affair to prepare many delicious *entrées*, such as chicken in shells (*en coquille*), or in papers (*en papillote*), and mushrooms in crust (*croûte aux champignons*).

For boiled fish the *sauce Hollandaise* is a decided success. In Paris every one speaks of this delicious sauce, and bribes the *chef de cuisine* for the receipt. It is made without stock, and is very simple.

For fried fish the perfection of accompaniments is the *sauce Tartare*—a mere addition of some capers, shallots, parsley, and pickles to the *sauce Mayonnaise*.

When tomatoes are so abundant, it is unpardonable that one should never serve a tomato sauce with a beefsteak, and a score of other meat dishes.

For a chicken or a lobster salad, learn unquestionably the *sauce Mayonnaise*.

In the thickening of sauces, let it be remembered that butter and flour should be well cooked together before the sauce is added, to prevent the flour from tasting uncooked. In butter sauces, however, only enough butter should be used to cook the flour, the remainder added, cut in pieces, after the sauce is taken from the fire. This preserves its flavor.

Drawn-butter Sauce.

Ingredients: Three ounces of butter, one ounce of flour, half a pint of water (or, better, white stock), and a pinch of salt and pepper.

Put two ounces of the butter into a stew-pan, and when it bubbles, sprinkle in the flour; stir it well with a wire egg-whisk until the flour is thoroughly cooked without taking color, and then mix in well the half-pint of water or stock. Take it off the fire, pass it through a sieve or gravy-strainer, and stir in the other ounce of butter cut in pieces. When properly mixed and melted, it is ready for use. This makes a pint of sauce.

Some persons like drawn-butter sauce slightly acid, in which case add a few drops of vinegar or lemon-juice just before serving.

Pickle Sauce.

Make a drawn-butter sauce; just before serving add two or three table-spoonfuls of pickled cucumbers chopped or minced very fine.

Boiled-egg Sauce.

Add to half a pint of drawn-butter sauce three hard-boiled eggs, chopped not too fine.

Caper Sauce.

Make a drawn-butter sauce—or, say, melt two ounces of butter in a saucepan; add a table-spoonful of flour; when the two are well mixed, add pepper and salt, and a little less than a pint of boiling water. Stir the sauce on the fire until it thickens, then add three table-spoonfuls of French capers. Removing the saucepan from the fire, stir into the sauce the yolk of an egg beaten with the juice of half a lemon.

Anchovy Sauce.

Add to half a pint of drawn-butter sauce two tea-spoonfuls of anchovy extract, or anchovy paste.

Shrimp Sauce.

To half a pint of drawn-butter sauce add one-third of a pint of picked boiled shrimps, whole, or chopped a little. Add at last moment a few drops of lemon-juice, and a very little Cayenne pepper. Let the sauce *simmer*, not boil. Some add a tea-spoonful of anchovy paste; more, perhaps, prefer it without the anchovy flavor.

Shrimps are generally sold at market already boiled. If they are not boiled, throw them into salted boiling water, and boil them until they are quite red. When cold, pick off the heads, and peel off the shells. Always save a few of the shrimps whole for garnishing the dish.

Lobster Sauce.

Before proceeding to make this sauce, break up the coral of the lobster, and put it on a paper in a slow oven for half an hour; then pound it in a mortar, and sprinkle it over the boiled fish when it is served. To prepare the sauce itself, chop the meat of the tail and claws of a good-sized lobster into pieces, not too small. Half an hour before dinner, make half a pint of drawn-butter sauce. Add to it the chopped lobster, a pinch of coral, a small pinch of Cayenne, and a little salt. An English lady says: "This process seems simple, yet nothing is rarer in cookery than good lobster sauce. The means of spoiling it are chiefly by chopping the lobster too small, or, worse, pounding it, inserting contents of the head, or using milk, or anchovy, or any sauces. It should not be a half-solid mass, or thin liquid, but the lobster should be distinct in a creamy bed."

Oyster Sauce.

Make a drawn-butter or white sauce; add a few drops of lemon or a table-spoonful of capers, or, if neither be at hand, a few drops of vinegar; add oysters strained from their liquor, and let them just come to a boil in the sauce.

This sauce is much better made with part cream, *i. e.*, used when making the drawn-butter sauce, instead of all water. In this case, do not add the lemon-juice or vinegar. Some make the white sauce of the oyster liquor, instead of water.

This sauce may be served in a sauce-boat, but it is nicer to pour it over the fish, boiled turkey, or chicken.

Parsley Sauce (*for Boiled Fish or Fowls*).

To half a pint of hot drawn-butter sauce add two table-spoonfuls of chopped parsley. The appearance of the sauce is improved by coloring it with a little spinach-green

Cauliflower Sauce (*for Boiled Poultry*).

Add boiled cauliflowers, cut into little flowerets, to a drawn-butter sauce made with part cream.

Lemon Sauce (*for Boiled Fowls*).

To half a pint of drawn-butter sauce add the inside of a lemon, chopped (seeds taken out), and the chicken liver boiled and mashed fine.

Chicken Sauce (*to serve with Boiled or Stewed Fowls*).

Put butter the size of an egg into a bright saucepan, and when it bubbles add a table-spoonful of flour; cook it, and add a pint, or rather less, of boiling water; when smooth, take it from the fire, and add the beaten yolks of two or three eggs, and a few drops of lemon-juice, pepper, and salt. Or, Stock can be used instead of boiling water, when two or three small slices of onion are placed in the butter after it begins to bubble, and then allowed to cook yellow; after the flour is cooked, stock is added instead of water, and when smooth, it is taken from the fire, a few drops of lemon-juice, pepper, and salt are added, and the sauce is strained through the gravy-strainer or sieve, to remove the pieces of onion.

Maître-d'hôtel Butter (*for Beefsteak, Broiled Meat, or Fish*).

Mix butter the size of an egg, the juice of half a lemon, and two or three sprigs of parsley, chopped very fine; pepper and salt all together. Spread this over any broiled meat or fish when hot; then put the dish into the oven a few moments, to allow the butter to penetrate the meat.

Mint Sauce (*for Roast Lamb*).

Put four table-spoonfuls of chopped mint, two table-spoonfuls of sugar, and a quarter of a pint of vinegar into the sauce-boat. Let it remain an hour or two before dinner, that the vinegar may become impregnated with the mint.

Currant-jelly Sauce (*for Venison*).

A simple sauce made of currant jelly melted with a little water is very nice; yet Francatelli's receipt is much better, viz.:

"Bruise half a stick of cinnamon and six cloves; put them into a stew-pan with one ounce of sugar and the peel of half a lemon, pared off very thin, and perfectly free from any portion of white pulp; moisten this with one and a half sherry-glassfuls of port-wine, and set the whole to gently simmer or heat on the stove for half an hour; then strain it into a small stew-pan containing half a glassful of currant jelly. Just before sending the sauce to the table, set it on the fire to boil, in order to melt the currant jelly, and so that it may mix with the essence of spice, etc."

Tomato Sauce (No. 1).

Stew six tomatoes half an hour with two cloves, a sprig of parsley, pepper, and salt; press this through a sieve; put a little butter into a saucepan over the fire, and when it bubbles add a heaping tea-spoonful of flour; mix and cook it well, and add the tomato-pulp, stirring until it is smooth and consistent.

Some add one or two slices of onion at first. It is a decided improvement to add three or four table-spoonfuls of stock; however, the sauce is very good without it, and people are generally too careless to have stock at hand.

Tomato Sauce (No. 2).

Ingredients: One-quart can of tomatoes, two cloves, one small sprig of thyme, two sprigs of parsley, half a small bay-leaf, three pepper-corns, three allspice, two slices of carrot (one and a half ounces), one-ounce onion (one small onion), one and a half ounces of butter (size of a pigeon's egg), one and a half ounces of flour (one table-spoonful).

Put the tomatoes over the fire with all the above ingredients but the butter and flour, and when they have boiled about twenty minutes strain them through a sieve. Make a *roux* by putting the butter into a stew-pan, and when it bubbles sprinkle in the flour, which let cook, stirring it well; then pour in the tomato-pulp; when it is well mixed, it is ready for use.

Sauce Hollandaise, or Dutch Sauce.

As this is one of the best sauces ever made for boiled fish, asparagus, or cauliflower, I will give two receipts. The first is Dubois'; the second is from the Cooking-school in New York. None should call themselves cooks unless they know how to make the *sauce Hollandaise*, and simple enough it is.

1st. "Pour four table-spoonfuls of good vinegar into a small stew-pan, and add some pepper-corns and salt; let the liquid boil until it is reduced to half; let it cool; then add to it the well-beaten yolks of four or five eggs, also four ounces (size of an egg) of good butter, more salt, if necessary, and a very little nutmeg. Set the stew-pan on a very slow fire, and stir the liquid until it is about as thick as cream; immediately remove it. Now put this stew-pan or cup into another pan containing a little warm water kept at the side of the fire. Work the sauce briskly with a spoon, or with a little whisk, so as to get it frothy, but adding little bits of butter, in all about three ounces" (*I* would say the size of half an egg). "When the sauce has become light and smooth, it is ready for use."

2d. "Put a piece of butter the size of a pigeon's egg into a saucepan, and when it bubbles stir in with an egg-whisk an even table-spoonful of flour; let it continue to bubble until the flour is thoroughly cooked, when stir in half a pint of boiling water, or, better, of veal stock; when it boils, take it from the fire, and stir into it gradually the beaten yolks of four eggs; return the sauce to the fire for a minute, to set the eggs, without allowing it to boil; again remove the sauce, stir in the juice of half a small lemon, and fresh butter the size of a walnut, cut into small pieces, to facilitate its melting, and stir all well with the whisk."

Mushrooms, for Garnish (*Gouffé*).

Separate the button part from the stalk; then peel them with a sharp knife, cutting off merely the skin. Put them into a stew-pan with a table-spoonful of lemon-juice and two table-spoonfuls of water. Toss them well, to impregnate them with the liquid. The object of the lemon-juice is to keep them white. Then put them on a sharp fire in boiling water, with some butter added. When they are boiled tender they are ready for use, *i. e.*, for garnishing and for sauces.

Mushroom Sauce (*to serve with Beefsteaks, Fillets of Beef, etc.*).

Having prepared the mushrooms by cutting off the stalks, and if they are large, by cutting them in halves or quarters, throw them into a little boiling water, or, what is much better, stock. Do not use more than is necessary to cover them. This must be seasoned with salt, pepper, and a little butter. Boil the mushrooms until they are tender, then thicken the gravy slightly with a *roux* of butter and flour. Add a few drops of lemon-juice. It is now ready to pour over the meat.

Mushroom White Sauce (*to serve with Boiled Fowls or with Cutlets*).

Prepare the mushrooms as for garnishing; boil them tender in rich white stock, made of veal or chicken; thicken with a *roux* of butter and flour, and add one or two table-spoonfuls of cream.

Mushroom Sauce (*made with Canned Mushrooms*).

Put a piece of butter the size of a walnut into a small stew-pan or tin basin, and when it bubbles add a tea-spoonful (not heaping) of flour; when well cooked, stir in a cupful of stock (reduced and strong), and half a tea-cupful of the mushroom-juice from the can; let it simmer for a minute or two; then, after straining it, add half or three quarters of a can of mushrooms, pepper, salt, and a few drops of lemon-juice. When thoroughly hot it is ready to pour over the meat.

A Simple Bechamel Sauce.

Put butter the size of a walnut into a stew-pan, and when it bubbles stir in an even table-spoonful of flour, which cook thoroughly without letting it take color. Mix into the *roux* a cupful of strong hot veal stock (*i. e.*, veal put into cold water and boiled four or five hours), a cupful of boiling cream, and one grating of nutmeg; let it simmer, stirring it well for a few minutes, then strain, and it is ready for use. The sauce would be improved if the usual soup-bunch vegetables were added to the stock while it is being made.

Bechamel Sauce.

Ingredients: One pint of veal stock (a knuckle of veal put into one gallon of cold water, boiled five hours, skimmed and strained), half an ounce of onion (quarter of a rather small one), quarter of an ounce of turnip (quarter of a turnip), one ounce of carrot (quarter of a good-sized carrot), half an ounce of parsley (two sprigs), quarter of a bay-leaf, half a sprig of thyme, three pepper-corns, half a lump of sugar, a small blade of mace.

Put one ounce (size of a walnut) of butter into a stew-pan, and when hot add to it all the above ingredients but the stock and the mace; fry this slowly until it assumes a yellow color; do not let it brown, as the sauce should be white when done; stir in now a table-spoonful (one ounce) of flour, which let cook a minute, and add the blade of mace and the stock (boiling) from another stew-pan. After it has all simmered about five minutes, strain it through a sieve without allowing the vegetables to pass through; return the strained sauce to the fire, reduce it by boiling about one-third, when add three or four table-spoonfuls of good thick cream, and the sauce is ready.

Sauce Aux Fines Herbes.

Ingredients: Half a pint of good stock, three table-spoonfuls of mushrooms, one table-spoonful of onions, two table-spoonfuls of parsley, and one shallot, all chopped fine. Fry the shallot and onion in a little butter until they assume a light-yellow color, then add a tea-spoonful of flour and cook it a minute; stir in the stock, mushrooms, and parsley, simmer for five minutes, then add a little Worcestershire sauce, and salt to taste. If no Worcestershire sauce is at hand, add pepper to taste in its place.

Sauce Tartare (*a Cold Sauce*).

To a scant half pint of *Mayonnaise* sauce (made with the mustard added) mix in two table-spoonfuls of capers, one small shallot (quarter of a rather small onion, a poor substitute), two gerkins (or two ounces of cucumber pickle), and one table-spoonful of parsley, all chopped *very* fine. This sauce will keep a long time, and is delicious for fried fish, fried oysters, boiled cod-fish, boiled tongue, or as dressing for a salad.

By making the following simple sauce, one can produce several by a little variation.

A Simple Brown Sauce.

Put into a saucepan a table-spoonful of minced onion and a little butter. When it has taken color, sprinkle in a heaping tea-spoonful of flour; stir well, and when brown add half a pint of stock. Cook it a few minutes, and strain. Now, by adding a cupful of claret, two cloves, a sprig of parsley, and one of thyme, a bay-leaf, pepper, and salt, and by boiling two or three minutes and straining it, one has the *sauce poivrade*.

If, instead of the claret, one should add to the *poivrade* sauce a table-spoonful each of minced cucumber pickles, vinegar, and capers, one has the *sauce piquante*.

By adding one tea-spoonful of made mustard, the juice of half a lemon, and a little vinegar to the *poivrade*, instead of the claret, one has the *sauce Robert*.

BEEF.

For a roast of beef, the sirloin and tenderloin cuts are considered the best. They are more expensive, and are no better than the best cuts of a rib roast: the sixth, seventh, and eighth ribs are the choicest cuts. The latter roasts are served to better advantage by requesting the butcher to remove the bones and roll the meat. Always have him send the bones also, as they are a valuable acquisition to the soup-pot. As the rolled rib roasts are shaved evenly off and across the top when carved (the roasts are to be cooked rare, of course), they present an equally good appearance for a second cooking. I have really served a roast a third time to good advantage, serving it the last time *à la jardinière*. Of course, in summer large cuts should not be purchased.

If the animal is young and large, and the meat is of clear, bright-red color, and the fat white, the meat is sure to be tender and juicy.

There is no better sauce for a good, juicy roast of beef than the simple juice of the meat. Horse-radish sauce may be served if the beef is not particularly good.

If a sauce is made by adding hot water, flour, pepper, and salt to the contents of the baking-pan after the beef is cooked, do not serve it with a half-inch depth of pure grease on top in the sauce-boat. This is as absurd, when it can be allowed to stand a moment and simply *poured off*, or taken off with a spoon, as to serve wet salt at table, which can easily be placed in the oven a few moments to dry, before sifting. Also, this kind of baking-pan sauce would not be so very objectionable, if cooks generally knew that it does not require a scientific education, nor a herculean effort, to strain it through a gravy-strainer.

To Roast or Bake Beef.

A few rules for roasting and baking beef: Allow nine minutes to the pound for *baking* a rolled rib-roast; for *roasting* it, allow ten minutes to the pound. Sirloin roasts require eight minutes to the pound for baking, nine minutes for roasting.

To bake, have the oven very hot. Before putting in the meat, sprinkle over pepper and salt, and dredge with flour. Pour a little boiling water into the pan before baking. Baste frequently.

To roast, have a bright fire. Hang the joint about eighteen inches from it at first, put a little clarified dripping into the dripping-pan, baste the meat with it when first prepared to cook, and every fifteen minutes afterward. Twenty minutes before the beef is done, sprinkle with pepper and salt, dredge with flour, baste with a little butter or dripping. Keep the fire bright, and turn the meat before it. It should be well browned and frothed. The cut, a rolled rib roast, with mashed potatoes.

Yorkshire Pudding.

Ingredients: Six large table-spoonfuls of flour, three eggs (well beaten), one salt-spoonful of salt, enough milk to make it of the consistency of soft custard (about one and a half pints).

Add enough milk to the flour and salt to make a smooth, stiff batter; add the eggs, and enough more milk to make it of the proper consistency. Beat all well together, pour it into a shallow pan (buttered); bake three-quarters of an hour.

Some empty the dripping-pan three-quarters of an hour before baked beef is done, and put the pudding into the empty pan, the beef on a three-cornered stand over it, that its juice may drop on the pudding. If beef is roasted, the pudding may be first baked in the oven, then placed under the beef for fifteen or twenty minutes, to catch any stray drops. It is as often served, though, baked in the oven in the ordinary way.

It is cut into squares and served on a hot plate, to be eaten with roast beef. It is a favorite English dish.

Beef à la Mode.

Six or seven pounds from a round of beef are generally selected; however, there is a cut from the shoulder which answers very well for an *à-la-mode beef*. If the round is used, extract the bone. Make several deep incisions into the meat with a thin sharp knife; press into most of them lardoons of pork about half an inch square, and two or three inches long; in the other cuts, and especially the one from whence the bone was extracted, stuff almost any kind of force-meat, the simplest being as follows: Mix some soaked bread with a little chopped beef-suet, onion, any herbs, such as parsley, thyme, or summer savory; a little egg, Cayenne pepper, salt, and cloves. Press the beef into shape, round or oval, and tie it securely.

Put trimmings of pork into the bottom of a large saucepan or iron pot, and when hot put over the meat; brown it all over by turning all sides to the bottom of the pot, which should now be uncovered. This will take about half an hour. Next sprinkle over a heaping table-spoonful of flour, and brown that also. Put a small plate under the beef, to prevent burning, and fill the pot with enough boiling water to half cover the meat; throw over a saucerful of sliced onions, carrots, some turnips, if you like, and some parsley. There are iron pots, with tight iron covers, which are made expressly for this kind of cooking; but if you have none of this description, you will now have to cover the one used with enough covers, towels, etc., to make it tight as possible, so that the meat may be cooked in the steam. Let it cook for four or five hours, never allowing the water to stop boiling. Watch it, that it may not get too low, and replenish it with boiling water. When the meat is done, put it on a hot platter; strain the gravy, skim off every particle of fat, add two or three table-spoonfuls of port or sherry wine, also pepper and salt, if necessary, and pour this gravy and selected pieces of the vegetables over the meat.

Baked onions placed around the beef as a garnish, complete the dish for a course at dinner.

BRAISED BEEF (No. 1).—*New York Cooking-school.*

Ingredients: Six-pound loin of beef, half a pound of pork, three-fourths of a cupful of flour, two-ounce onion (one small onion), three-ounce carrot (half a large carrot), one-ounce turnip, one-third of a bunch of parsley, one sprig of thyme, two cloves, three allspice, six pepper-corns, half of a bay-leaf.

Trim the beef into a shapely piece; stick a knife quite through different portions of it, in which apertures press slices or lardoons of pork, half an inch square, and three or four inches long. Tie the beef into shape with twine. Lay scraps of pork on the bottom of a saucepan, place it on a brisk fire, and when hot put in the beef; brown it all over by turning the different sides to the bottom of the uncovered saucepan. It will take about half an hour to brown it. Now sprinkle over the beef three-fourths of a cupful of flour (three ounces), also the vegetables and spices; and brown all this by again turning the meat over the fire. When they are of fine color, pour over a tumblerful of claret, which reduce to half; then fill the saucepan with boiling stock or water; cover it tightly, and place it in a hot oven for two and a half hours. When done, put the beef on a hot platter.

Strain the sauce in which the beef was cooked, take off every particle of fat, season with more salt, if necessary; pour about half a cupful of it over the beef in the platter, and serve the remainder in a sauce-boat.

The beef may be surrounded with green pease, prepared as follows: Wash a can of American pease in cold water, then put them over the fire with half a cupful of boiling water, salt, pepper, one ounce of butter, and one salt-spoonful of sugar. When the pease have simmered a minute, strain them from their liquor, and place them in the platter around the beef.

Braised Beef (No. 2).

The same cut which is used for an *à-la-mode* beef may be braised in the same manner as is described for a fillet of beef braised. This may be served with the gravy, as is there described, or with the addition of the *jardinière* of vegetables.

Braised Beef, with Horse-radish Sauce.

Braise five pounds of fresh beef (not too lean), with an onion and a carrot sliced, two or three sprigs of parsley, four or five cloves, a little celery, if you have it, pepper, salt, and about a quart of boiling water. Cover it tightly, and let it cook about three hours, replenishing with a little boiling water, if the steam escapes too much.

Sauce.—Simmer together for quarter of an hour half a cupful of grated cracker, half a cupful of grated horse-radish, one cupful of cream, a table-spoonful of the fat from the top of the water in which the beef is cooked, salt, and pepper.

Place the beef on the platter in which it is to be served, and pour the sauce around it. Garnish with parsley.

Fillet of Beef.

I will be very specific about the fillet of beef, as it is easily managed at home, and is very expensive ordered from the *restaurateur*. His price is generally ten dollars for a dressed and cooked fillet of beef for a dinner for ten or twelve persons. To buy it from the butcher costs a dollar a pound when dressed; three pounds are quite sufficient for ten or twelve persons. To lard it (an affair of ten minutes) would cost ten cents more; a box of French canned mushrooms, an additional forty cents; a little stock, five cents.

One sees a fillet of beef at almost every dinner party. "That same fillet, with mushrooms," a frequent diner-out will say. I hope to see it continued, for among the substantials there is nothing more satisfactory.

A good butcher will always deliver a fillet of beef already dressed; if, however, it is necessary to have it dressed at home, the *modus operandi* is as follows:

To Trim a Fillet of Beef.

The fillet is the under side of the loin of beef. The steaks cut from this part are called porter-house-steaks. This under side, or fillet, is covered with skin and fat. "All the skin and fat must be removed from the top of the fillet, from one end to the other; then the rib-bones are disengaged. The fat adhering to the side opposite the ribs is only partially removed. Now the sinewy skin covering the upper meat of the fillet must be removed in strips, proceeding by slipping the blade of the knife between the skin and the meat. This operation is very simple; yet it requires great precision. The upper part of a trimmed fillet must be smooth, *i. e.*, must not be furrowed by hollows occasioned by wrong movements of the knife. The skin being removed, both extremities of the fillet are rounded. The fat inside the rib is the only portion of fat allowed to adhere to the meat. The larding of the meat is applied to its upper surface."

To Cook a Fillet of Beef.

After it is trimmed and larded, put it into a small baking-pan, in the bottom of which are some chopped pieces of pork and beef-suet; sprinkle some salt and pepper over it, and put a large ladleful of hot stock into the bottom of the pan, or it may be simply basted with boiling water. Half an hour (if the oven is very hot, as it should be) before dinner, put it into the oven. Baste it often, supplying a little hot stock, if necessary.

French cooks often braise a fillet of beef. I do not like it as well as baking or roasting, as the vegetables and wine destroy the beef's own flavor.

To Make the Mushroom Sauce.

Take a ladleful of stock, free from grease, from the stock-pot; add to it part of the juice from the can of mushrooms; thicken it with a little flour and butter mixed (*roux*); add pepper, salt, and a few drops of lemon-juice; now add the mushrooms—let them simmer a few minutes. Pour the sauce over the fillet of beef, and serve.

At small dinner companies, where the host carves, or has a good carver, the fillet can be served entire, decorated as elaborately as one wishes. If, however, the dinner is served from the side, it is convenient to have it carved as shown in cut on preceding page. The centre of the fillet is disengaged, then carved, and returned to its place. It has then the appearance of being whole.

To Garnish a Fillet of Beef.

As I have mentioned before, a fillet of beef is generally served with mushrooms; sometimes with different vegetables *à la jardinière*; sometimes with French pease; sometimes with potatoes cut into little round balls, and fried in boiling lard, called potatoes *à la Parisienne* on a French bill of fare; sometimes with stuffed tomatoes; sometimes skewers are put in stuck through a turnip carved into a cup, and this cup holds horse-radish. But some people say skewers remind them of steamboat cooking; then some people are not easily pleased, anyway; and who remembers of having seen so many skewers on steamboats, after all? Not that I am particularly advocating skewers, but I think dishes *taste* better, as a general thing, when they are decorated in almost any manner. I once saw at a dinner in Paris hot slices of roast or baked fillet of beef, tastefully arranged on a platter, with *sauce Hollandaise* (rather thick) poured over each slice in the form of a ring. It was a success.

The manner of garnishing a fillet of beef *à la Godard* and *à la Provençale*, etc., with truffles, *quenelles*, livers, olives, etc., all stewed with wines, stocks, etc., I will not explain. It is enough to make one groan to think of learning to make them, and more than ever to eat them.

To Roast a Fillet of Beef.

Lard it, and bind it carefully to the skewer with a small wire; cover the fillet with sweet salad-oil and a little lemon-juice. Do not place it too near the fire at first, as it would scorch the larding. Baste it frequently.

A professional cook would glaze the fillet two or three times with a glazing-brush, beginning the first time about five minutes before taking it away from the fire, then glazing it again when it is on the dish to be served.

Glaze is merely strong stock boiled down until it is almost a thick jelly. When the fillet is carved at table, the little juice which falls into the dish should be poured over each of the slices.

To Braise a Fillet of Beef.

Put the larded fillet into a braising-pan or stew-pan; put in trimmings of pork, onions (with some cloves stuck in), carrots, a little celery (all cut in thick slices), and a bunch of parsley. Salt the meat slightly. Pour in stock and white wine, so that it may reach to half the height of the beef. If a braising-pan is used, cover the meat with a well-buttered paper, as in that case live coals are put on top of the pan. If you use a stew-pan, simply cover it as tight as possible. Let it simmer, replenishing it, when necessary, with more boiling stock. It will require an hour or an hour and a half to cook. When done, drain it: a professional cook would glaze it. Put it into the oven a moment to dry the larding. Pass the cooking-stock through a sieve; skim off the fat; add some tomato sauce; let it boil until it is reduced to the degree requisite. Serve the fillet whole, or carved in slices ready to serve. Generally only the middle part of the fillet is used, as the whole fillet is quite large—weighing from eight to ten pounds.

To Trim With Vegetables (*à la Jardinière*).

Every kind of vegetable is used, such as potatoes, carrots, turnips, beets, small onions, cauliflower-blossoms, asparagus-heads, French beans, pease, etc. The larger vegetables are cut into little fancy shapes with a vegetable-cutter or a fluted knife, or with a little plain knife, into little balls, olives, squares, diamonds, or into any form to suit the taste. Each kind of vegetable should be boiled separately in salted water or stock. The vegetables are piled into little groups, each pile being of one kind of vegetable.

Fillet of Beef cut into Slices or Scollops.

This is a good way of managing the beef that is left from the roast or baked fillet of beef to be served the second day. Cut the fillet, after reheating it in the oven, into slices about three-fourths of an inch thick, and two inches wide. Form a circle in a dish by lapping each of these scollops partly over the other. Fill the centre with a tomato sauce, or potatoes *à la Parisienne*, or mushrooms, or with any of the small vegetables, such as pease, beans, little balls of carrots, potatoes, etc., in different little piles; or with truffles (they can be procured canned) sliced, with Madeira sauce; or with mushrooms and truffles mixed, with Madeira sauce.

Beefsteak.

The porter-house and tenderloin steaks are best. Of course, there is great difference in the different cuts of these steaks. For a cheap steak, a good cut of what is called chuck-steak is best. It has more flavor and juice, and is more tender than the round-steak, costing the same price.

Have the choice steaks cut half an inch thick at least; they are even better three-quarters of an inch thick. Grease the gridiron well with pork or beef-suet. Have it quite hot. Put on the steak over a hot, clear fire; cover it with a baking-pan. In a moment, when the steak is colored, turn it over. Watch it constantly, turning it whenever it gets a little brown. Do not stick the fork into the middle of the steak, only into the sides, where it will do least harm by letting out the juice. It should be quite rare or pink in the centre, though not *raw*. When cooked enough, put it on a hot platter; sprinkle over plenty of salt and pepper—mind not to put on the salt and pepper before the steak is cooked; then spread over the top some sweet, fresh butter. Set the platter in the oven a few moments, to let the butter soak a little in the steak; then serve it immediately. Do not use too much butter; there should be none at all, or at least only a few stray drops, in the bottom of the platter. There should be no gravy. The juice of a properly cooked steak is supposed to be in the inside of the steak, and not swimming in the dish.

A steak is much improved by a simple addition, called by professional cooks *à la maître d'hôtel*.

When the steak is cooked, it is placed on the hot platter. First, then, salt and pepper are sprinkled over; then comes a sprinkling of very finely chopped parsley; then some drops of lemon-juice; lastly, small pieces of butter are carefully spread over. Place the steak into the oven for a few moments until the butter is well melted and soaked into the steak.

For extra-company breakfasts, only the fillets, *i. e.*, the tender parts of the porter-house or tenderloin steaks, are used. They are cut into little even shapes, round or oval, one for each plate. They are cooked, then served in a hot dish, surrounded with Saratoga potatoes, or fried potatoes in any form, or with water-cresses, or with mushrooms, or stuffed tomatoes, or green pease, etc.

Corned Beef.

A good piece of beef well corned, then well boiled, is a most excellent dish.

Put it into the pot with enough cold water to just cover it. When it comes to a boil, set it on the back of the range, so that it will boil moderately. Too fast boiling renders meat tough, yet the water should never be allowed to cease boiling until the meat is done; skim often. Let it boil at least four or five hours, according to its size. It must be thoroughly done. In England, where this dish is an especial favorite, carrots are always boiled and served with the beef. The carrot flavor improves the meat, and the meat improves the carrot. Do not put the carrots into the pot, however, until there is only time for them to become thoroughly cooked before serving (about three-quarters of an hour). Serve the carrots around the beef.

In America, cabbage is oftener boiled with corned beef. This is very nice also. If cabbage is used, add at the same time one or two little red peppers. When about to serve, press out all the water from the cabbage, adding little pieces of butter. Serve the meat placed in the centre of the cabbage.

Little pickles are a pretty garnish for corned beef, with or without the vegetables.

Corned Beef to serve Cold (*Mrs. Gratz Brown*).

If it is too salt, soak it for an hour in cold water, then put it over the fire, covered with fresh cold water, four or five cloves (for about six pounds of beef), and three table-spoonfuls of molasses. Boil it slowly. In an hour change the water, adding five more cloves and three more table-spoonfuls of molasses. In two hours more, press the beef, after removing the bones, into a basin rather small for it; then, turning it over, place a flat-iron on top. When entirely cold, the beef is to be sliced for lunch or tea.

Beefsteak Stewed.

Never use a choice steak for a stew. Stewing is only a good way of cooking an inferior steak. The meat from a soup-bone would make a very good stew.

Put ripe tomatoes (peeled and cut) into a stew-pan; sprinkle over pepper and salt. Let them cook a little to make some juice; put in the pieces of beef, some little pieces of butter mixed with flour, two or three cloves, and no water. Let it stew until the meat is quite done. Then press the tomatoes through a sieve. Serve all on the same dish.

Beefsteak Rolled.

Procure a round steak, spread over it a layer of almost any kind of force-meat. An ordinary bread, onion, thyme, or parsley dressing, used to stuff turkeys, is very good. Begin, then, at one end of the steak, and roll it carefully; tie the roll to keep it in shape. Bake it in the oven as you would a turkey, basting very often. Make a gravy of the drippings, adding water, flour, and a little butter mixed; season with pepper and salt, strain, skim off the fat, and pour it around the meat when served. Slice it neatly off the end when carving.

Beef Roll (*Cannelon de Bœuf*).

Chop two pounds of lean beef very fine; chop and pound in a mortar half a pound of fat bacon, and mix it with the beef. Season it with pepper and salt (it will not require much salt), a small nutmeg, the grated rind of a lemon, the juice of a quarter of it, a heaping table-spoonful of parsley minced fine; or it can be seasoned with an additional table-spoonful of onion; or, if no onion or parsley is at hand, with summer savory and thyme. Bind all these together with two eggs. Form them into a roll; surround the roll with buttered paper, which tie securely around it. Then cover it with a paste made of flour and water. Bake two hours. Remove the paper and crust. Serve it hot, with tomato-sauce or brown gravy. This may be made with raw or under-dressed meat. If the meat is not raw, but under-dressed, surround the roll with pie-crust. Bake, and serve with tomato-sauce, or any of the brown sauces, poured in the bottom of the dish. Potato *croquettes* may be served around it.

What to do with Cold Cooked Beef.

There is a good-sized book written on this subject. When there are about two hundred ways of utilizing cold cooked beef, one should not regard it contemptuously. I studied this treatise, and practiced from it, but soon considered the few old ways the best, after all. *Croquettes* are very good, and there are beef-sausages, or cakes, seasoned in different ways; beef rolls, meat pies, and mince-pies, made from a few scraps of cold cooked beef, are all exceedingly nice when properly made.

Beef Hash.

Notwithstanding this distinguished dish is so much abused, I particularly like it; not swimming hash, nor onion hash, nor Southern or Western hash, nor yet hash half cooked, but New York hash. I know a New York family who set a most expensive and elaborate table, which table is especially noted for its good hash. Large joints are purchased with special reference to this dish. Cold corned beef is generally considered best. The hash to which I have referred, however, is generally made of cold roast beef.

Chop the cold cooked meat rather fine; use half as much meat as of boiled potatoes (chopped when cold). Put a little boiling water and butter into an iron saucepan; when it boils again, put in the meat and potatoes well salted and peppered. Let it cook well, stirring it occasionally—not enough to make a *purée* or mush of it. It is not done before there is a coating at the bottom of the saucepan, from which the hash will free itself without sticking. The hash must not be at all watery, nor yet too dry, but so that it will stand quite firm on well-trimmed and buttered slices of toast, and to be thus served on a platter. *Voilà!*

Chicken or turkey hash should be made in the same way.

Meat Pie (*French Cook*).

Cut cold cooked meat into quite small dice; add pepper, salt, a little nutmeg, and two or three sprigs of chopped parsley; also a little thyme and a piece of bay-leaf, if you have them, but the two latter herbs may be omitted. Put a little butter into a saucepan, and when hot throw in a table-spoonful of flour, which brown carefully; pour in then several table-spoonfuls of hot water, or, better, stock; mix well; then introduce the meat dice; stir all well over the fire, cooking it thoroughly. Just before taking it up, mix in one or two eggs. It should be quite moist, yet consistent. Put a thin pie-crust into a pudding-dish. Fill in a few table-spoonfuls of the mixture; then lay on it a thin strip of bacon; continue these layers until the dish is filled. Now fit a piece of crust over the top; turn the edges in a fancy manner, and make a cut in the centre. Take a strip of pie-paste, form it into a tie or knot, wet the bottom, and place it over the cut in the centre of the pie, so as not to obstruct the opening.

The proper way to make a meat pie is with a pie-mold
Butter the mold, press the crust neatly around in the inside and bottom, and continue, as explained for the pudding-dish. When baked, the wire holding the sides of the mold is drawn out, and the mold removed from the pie. This pie can be made with veal or lamb, in the same manner.

MEAT RISSOLES.

For *rissoles*, cold beef, chicken, veal, tongue, or lamb may be used, separately or mixed. The meat should not be chopped, but cut into quite small dice. It is well to add to it a slight flavoring of chopped pork, and a little finely chopped parsley. As the meat can be prepared in different ways, the addition of a superfluous mushroom or two, cut into dice, would not be amiss.

Put a small piece of butter, size of a pigeon's egg, into a saucepan, and when it begins to boil add a heaping tea-spoonful of flour; stir for a minute to cook the flour, then add three or four table-spoonfuls of boiling water, or, what is much better, stock, gravy, or brown or white sauce if you happen to have it; when well mixed, add about two cupfuls of the meat dice, heat well, and just before taking from the fire stir in an egg.

The scraps of puff-paste are generally preferred, yet any kind of pie-paste may be used for *rissoles*. Roll the paste quite thin (one-sixth of an inch); wet it about three inches from the edge, and place upon it little balls (a generous tea-spoonful in each one) of the prepared meat, at distances of four inches apart; now lap over the edge of the paste, quite covering the balls of meat; press the side of the hand between each one, and, with the edge of a tumbler or muffin-ring, press the paste close to the meat; with a biscuit-cutter (scolloped one prettier) cut out each enveloped ball of meat into half circles. Now cut off the rough edges of the remaining paste, and proceed to make other rows of the *rissoles* in the same manner. With a brush wet all the tops with the yolk of an egg. Bake the *rissoles* in a hot oven, and serve them hot on a folded napkin. If they get cold, they may be reheated just before serving.

Beef or any Cold-meat Sausages.

Chop cold cooked beef very fine; add a fifth as much pork, also chopped fine; pepper, salt, a little sage, or any herbs preferred, lemon-juice, and a few sprinkles of flour; mix all together with an egg, or eggs; form into little balls, fry in butter or lard in a *sauté* pan. These sausages are good for breakfast served around a centre of apple-sauce. Or,

For Rice and Meat Cakes,

make as in last receipt, adding a very little butter. Stir in a quarter or half of its quantity of boiled rice; or, on another occasion, bread-crumbs may be substituted for rice.

Beef Croquettes.

[Image unavailable.]

There is no more satisfactory manner of using cold cooked beef than for *croquettes*, which may be served with tomato or any of the brown sauces, or may be served without sauce at all, as is generally the case. They are made in the same manner as is described for chicken *croquettes* merely substituting the same amount of beef for the chicken, and of rice for the brains.

A Cheap Arrangement.

Purchase two soup bones (twenty cents). Boil them four or five hours with a few vegetables   The stock will make two or three soups. Cut up the meat for *croquettes*. Of course the *croquettes* are better made with the best of meat, yet may be excellent when made of the soup meat.

Mince-pies (*made from Remnants of Cold Beef*).

A good disposition in winter of cold roast beef is to make with it two or three mince-pies, as by the following receipt: One cupful of chopped meat (quarter of it fat), two cupfuls of apple, one tea-spoonful of salt, one table-spoonful of ground allspice, half a table-spoonful of ground cinnamon, half a table-spoonful of ground cloves, one cupful of sugar, half a cupful of raisins, half a cupful of currants, one cupful of cider; or, if one has no cider, use the same amount of cider-vinegar and water mixed—say half of each.

A Common Pot-pie of Veal, Beef, or Chicken.

Cut the meat into pieces, and put them into enough boiling water to cover them well; add also two or three strips of pork. Cover the pot closely. Boil an hour, then season with pepper and salt to taste, and a little piece of butter.

Just before taking out the ingredients of the pot to send to table, put into it, when the water is boiling, separate spoonfuls of batter made with two eggs well beaten, two and a half or three cupfuls of buttermilk, one tea-spoonful of soda, and sufficient flour. The batter should be made just before it is cooked. It takes about three or four minutes to cook it, the water not to be allowed to stop boiling. The dish should then be served immediately, or the dumplings will become heavy.

Calf's Heart.

If people generally knew how nice a calf's heart is, if properly cooked, the butchers would never charge so little as ten cents for it. In France, the calf's heart and kidneys are considered great delicacies. In America they are often thrown away.

Merely wash off the blood. One could, by soaking, extract all the flavor from the heart. Stuff it with a veal force-meat stuffing, or a common stuffing, often used for turkeys, of bread-crumbs, onion, a little thyme or sage, egg, pepper, and salt. Tie a buttered paper over the mouth of the heart to keep the stuffing in place. Put it into a small baking-pan with a little hot water, pepper, and salt. Bake nearly two hours, basting it very frequently. When done, thicken the gravy with flour; strain, skim, and season it, and pour it on the dish around the heart. Garnish the plate with onions, first boiled until nearly done, then seasoned with pepper, salt, and a little butter, and browned in the oven.

Tongue, With Mustard Pickle Sauce.

Cut boiled tongue into slices; fry them in a little hot butter, with a sprinkle of minced onion thrown in. Then, for the sauce, take out the slices of tongue; put in a tea-spoonful of flour, and when brown, a tea-cupful of hot water. When done, strain, and season with salt and pepper; add a tablespoonful of chopped pickles (piccalilli is best); however, common cucumber pickles may be used, with a little mustard added; or the sauce may be flavored with capers, or with both capers and pickles. Let the slices of tongue soak in the sauce until ready to serve, then arrange the slices of tongue on a platter, one lapped over the other, and pour over the sauce. A beef tongue may be braised, and served with spinach or *sauce Tartare*, as described for sheep's tongues.

Tongue Slices, with Spinach and Sauce Tartare.

Braise the tongue as described for sheep's tongues (see page 158): arrange a circle of the slices around a platter, and on each slice smooth a little hill (enough for one person) of spinach prepared as described in the same receipt for "sheep's tongues with spinach." Put either a spoonful of *sauce Tartare* or a slice of lemon into or on the top of each spinach-mold. This makes a nice lunch or dinner dish.

VEAL.

The best pieces of veal are the loin and the fillet. A variety of dishes can be made with veal cutlets and their different accompaniments. Veal is always better cooked with pork or ham. Professional cooks generally trim and lard their veal cutlets, serving them with tomato-sauce, pease, beans, breakfast bacon, lemon-slices, cucumbers, etc. For a cheap dish, one of the most satisfactory is a knuckle of veal made into a ragout, or pot-pie. Any of the inferior cuts may be made into a *blanquette*.

A *fricandeau* of veal is perhaps considered the most distinguished veal dish. I would always advise the trimming of veal cutlets. It gives little trouble, but the appearance is much improved, and the trimmings should be thrown into the stock-pot. Veal should always be thoroughly cooked.

Roast of Veal—the Fillet.

Take out the bone of the joint; make a deep incision between the fillet and the flap; then fill it with stuffing made as follows: Two cupfuls of bread-crumbs, half a cupful of chopped pork, half a lemon-peel grated, a little juice, thyme, summer savory, or any herbs to taste; or it may be filled with a veal stuffing   Bind the veal into a round form, fasten it with skewers and twine, sprinkle over pepper and salt, and cover it with buttered paper. Be careful not to put the meat too near the fire at first. Baste well and often. Just before it is done, remove the paper, sprinkle over a little flour, and rub over it a little butter. This will give a frothy appearance to the surface of the meat. When done, put the pan of gravy on the fire; add a little flour, some boiling water, and, when cooked, some lemon-juice. Strain it, remove the grease, and pour it around the roast. Fry some pieces of ham cut in diamond shape; place these in a circle around the roast, each piece alternated with a slice of lemon.

A Fricandeau of Veal.

What is called a *fricandeau* of veal is simply a cushion of veal trimmed into shape, larded, and braised. Cut a thick slice (three or four pounds) from a fillet of veal, trim it around as in cut for "blind hare"   and lard it on top. Put some pieces of pork into a braising-kettle, or saucepan, if you have no braising-kettle; also slices of carrot, an onion with cloves stuck in, a stick of celery, and some parsley. Put in the meat, sprinkle over pepper and salt, and cover it with well-buttered paper. Now fill the pan with boiling stock, or water enough to just cover the meat. Put on a tight lid. If it is a braising-pan, set it upon the fire, with live coals on top. If a common saucepan, cover it, and put it into a hot oven.

It will take about two hours, or two hours and a half, to cook it. A professional cook would boil down the stock in which the *fricandeau* was cooked until reduced to a glaze, then with a brush would glaze all the top of the meat, placing it in the oven a moment to dry. However, it tastes as well without this extra trouble.

The best sauce for a *fricandeau* is a tomato-sauce. It is as often garnished with green pease, spinach, or sorrel; or a little wine (Madeira, port, or sherry) and *roux* may be added to the braising-stock for a gravy. The gravy should be strained, of course.

Veal Cutlets, Broiled.

The rib cutlets should always be neatly trimmed, the bone scraped at the end, so that it will look smooth and white. Broil them on a moderate fire, basting them occasionally with butter, and turning them often. Dish them in a circle with tomato-sauce.

Veal Cutlets, Sautéd and Fried.

These are cutlets cut from the round, although any veal cutlets may be cooked in the same way. Cut them into equal-sized pieces, beat them a little with a knife to get them into shape; season, egg, and bread-crumb them. Now, fry in a *sauté* pan, or rather *sauté* some thin slices of ham in a little hot lard, and when done take them out on a hot dish; fry slowly the cutlets in the same fat, and when done pour out some of the fat, if there is more than a tea-spoonful; add a little flour, then a little hot water, and, when cooked a few moments, season it well with lemon-juice, adding pepper and salt to taste; then strain it. Serve the cutlets in the centre of a dish, with the gravy poured over; and place alternate slices of the ham and lemon in a circle around them.

They are also very good *sautéd* in a little lard, and served with a cream gravy poured over; or they are nice egged (with a little chopped parsley and onion mixed with the egg), and bread-crumbed, and fried in hot lard.

Veal Cutlets, Braised.

Professional cooks usually braise veal cutlets. They lard them (an easy matter) all on the same side, the flavor of pork particularly well suiting veal. To proceed then: Mince some onions and carrots; put them in the bottom of a stew-pan; put the cutlets on this layer; cover well with stock (add wine if you choose), and let them cook until thoroughly done.

If you wish to be particular, boil down the stock and glaze them; or make a gravy of the stock with flour, *roux*, pepper and salt, and strain it; or serve them with tomato-sauce; or make a little round hill of mashed potatoes, and put the cutlets around; or serve with them, instead, beans, pease, or flowerets of cauliflowers.

Mutton or Veal Chops (*en papillote*).

Trim the chops; broil them in the usual way over the coals, and when done place each one in a paper (well buttered) cut in the form of Fig. 1; pour over each chop a sauce made as follows: For three cutlets thicken a cupful of strong broth with equal quantities of either cold cooked chicken, lamb, or veal, and mushrooms (the mushrooms are a great improvement to the dish, yet they may be omitted if more convenient) with a quarter proportion of cold boiled ham added, and also one or two sprigs of parsley, all chopped very fine. Pour this hot over the hot cutlets; place a *very thin* slice of fat salt pork over each cutlet; place them in a hot oven for about ten minutes. Serve *immediately* while the chops are steaming hot.

Blanquette of Veal (*French Cook*).

Cut any kind of veal (say two pounds) into pieces; put it into boiling water, with a little bulb of garlic or slice of onion, and when done throw the meat from the boiling water into cold water, to whiten it. This is the rule, but I usually dispense with it. Make a drawn butter sauce, *i. e.*, put butter the size of an egg into a saucepan, and when it bubbles mix in a tablespoonful of flour, which cook a minute, without letting it color; add then two cupfuls of boiling water and a little nutmeg. When the veal is done, drain it from the water, and let it simmer several minutes in the sauce, adding at the same time a sprig of parsley chopped fine. When just ready to serve, place the pieces of meat on a hot platter; stir the yolks of three eggs into the sauce without allowing them to boil; also several drops, or a seasoning, of lemon-juice. Pour the sauce over the veal, and serve.

BLIND HARE (*Mrs. Charles Parsons*).

Ingredients: Three pounds of minced veal, three pounds of minced beef, eight eggs well beaten, three stale rolls, or the same amount of bread-crumbs, pepper, salt, two grated nutmegs, a heaping table-spoonful of ground cinnamon. Mix all well together. Form it into an oval-shaped loaf, smooth it, and sprinkle bread or cracker crumbs over the top. Bake it in a moderate oven about three hours. It is to be sliced when cold.

BEWITCHED VEAL (*Mrs. Judge Embry*).

Ingredients: Three pounds of lean veal, half a pound of fat salt pork, one nutmeg grated, one small onion, butter the size of an egg, a little red pepper, and salt.

Chop all very fine, and mix them together, with three eggs well beaten, and a tea-cupful of milk; form it into a small loaf, pressing it very firmly; cover it with fine bread-crumbs; bake two hours and a half. It is intended to be eaten cold, yet is very good hot. The slices may be served in a circle around salad.

PLAIN VEAL STEW OR POT-PIE.

Cut the meat from a knuckle of veal into pieces not too small; put them into a pot with some small pieces of salt pork, and plenty of pepper and salt; pour over enough hot water to cover it well, and let it boil until the meat is *thoroughly* done; then, while the water is still boiling, drop in (by the spoonful) a batter made with the following ingredients: Two eggs well beaten, two and a half or three cupfuls of buttermilk, one even tea-spoonful of soda, and flour enough to make a thick batter. Cover the pot, and as soon as the batter is well cooked, serve it. By standing, it becomes heavy.

TO COOK LIVER (*Melanie Lourant*), No. 1.

Put a little lard into a saucepan, and when hot throw in half an onion minced fine, one or two sprigs of parsley, chopped, and the slices of calf's liver. Turn the liver several times, allowing it to cook well and imbibe the taste of the onion and parsley. When cooked, place it at the side of the fire. In another saucepan make a sauce as follows: Put in a piece of butter size of a large hickory-nut, and when it bubbles sprinkle in a heaping tea-spoonful of flour; stir it until it assumes a fine brown color, then pour in a cupful of boiling water, stirring it well with the egg-whisk; add pepper, salt, a table-spoonful of vinegar, and a heaping table-spoonful of capers. The sauce is very nice without the capers, but very much improved with them. Drain out the slices of liver, which put into the sauce, and let them remain at the side of the fire until ready to serve. Chopped pickle may be substituted for the capers, and stock may be used instead of the boiling water.

TO COOK LIVER (No. 2).

Fry in a *sauté* pan some thin slices of breakfast bacon, and when done put them on a hot dish; fry then thin slices of liver in the same fat, which have previously been thrown into boiling water for only a *moment*, and then been sprinkled with flour. When well done on both sides, serve them and the bacon on the same dish, and garnish them with slices of lemon.

CALF'S BRAINS.

Before cooking, remove the fibrous membranes around them. Throw them into a pint of cold water, in which are mixed half a tea-spoonful of salt and one tea-spoonful of vinegar; boil them three minutes, then plunge them into cold water. When cold and about to be served, cut them into scollops; and when seasoned with pepper and salt, egged, and bread-crumbed, *sauté* them in a little hot butter. Serve with tomato-sauce. Or they may be served with *spighetti* (a small macaroni) cooked with tomato-sauce
and placed around them, when they are called brains *à la Milanaise*.

SWEET-BREADS.

Veal sweet-breads are best. They spoil very soon. The moment they come from market, they should be put into cold water, to soak for about an hour; lard them, or rather draw a lardoon of pork through the centre of each sweet-bread, and put them into salted boiling water, or, better, stock, and let them boil about twenty minutes, or until they are thoroughly done; throw them then into cold water for only a few moments. They will now be firm and white. Remove carefully the skin and little pipes, and put them in the coolest place until ready to cook again. The simplest way to cook them is the best one, as follows:

Fried Sweet-breads.

Parboil them as just explained. Just before serving, cut them in even-sized pieces, sprinkle over pepper and salt, egg and bread-crumb them, and fry them in hot lard. They are often immersed in boiling lard, yet oftener fried in the *sauté* pan. If *sautéd*, when done put them on a hot dish, turn out part of the lard from the *sauté* pan, leaving about half a tea-spoonful; pour in a cupful of milk thickened with a little flour; let it cook, stirring it constantly, and season it with pepper and salt; strain, and pour over the sweet-breads. With green pease, serve without sauce. This is the usual combination at dinner or breakfast companies, the pease in the centre of the dish, and the sweet-breads around (see cut above). Or they are often served whole with cauliflower or asparagus heads, when the cream-sauce is poured over both; or they are also nice piled in the centre of a dish, with macaroni (cooked with cheese) placed around them like a nest, and browned a little with a salamander (see cut on next page), or with a tomato-sauce in the centre of the dish, and the sweet-breads around, or with stuffed tomatoes alternating with the sweet-breads on the dish, or with mushrooms in the centre, or served on a dish made of boiled rice, called a rice *casserole*

or in little rice molds called *cassolettes*. To make the latter, boil the rice well, then work it to a smooth paste with a spoon; fill some little buttered patty-pans with the rice, and when it is quite cold take it out, brush the *cassolettes* with butter on the outside, and color them a little in a hot oven; scoop out the inside, leaving the rice crust a quarter of an inch thick. Fill the *cassolettes* with the sweet-breads cut into pieces, and pour over each a spoonful of cream dressing; or they may be *sautéd* as described, and served with a *maître-d'hôtel* sauce poured over.

Sweet-breads à la Milanaise.

Sweet-breads fried as in preceding receipt are placed in the centre of a hot platter. Small piped macaroni broken into two or three inch lengths is cooked with tomatoes as in receipt   and neatly arranged in a circle around them.

Sweet-breads Larded and Braised (*English Lady*).

Trim all the skin and cartilage very carefully from two fine sweet-breads; lay them in cold water for an hour, and lard them; lay some slices of bacon in the bottom of a braising-pan, or any pan with a good cover (Francatelli would add also minced onions, carrots, celery, and parsley; however, they are quite good enough without); then put in sweet-breads, with slices of bacon between the pan and the sweet-breads; pour over all some stock, just high enough not to touch the larding, which must stand up free; let it simmer very gently for half or three-quarters of an hour. Look at it occasionally to see that the stock does not waste; add a little if it does. When done, hold a salamander or a hot kitchen shovel over the sweet-breads until they are a pale-yellow color on top. Serve these with tomato-sauce poured in the centre of the dish. The whole dish should look moist, the sweet-breads nearly white, and the larding transparent, standing up distinct and firm, like glass, white at the bottom, and pale-yellow on top.

BAKED SWEET-BREADS (*New York Cooking-school*).

Put a pair of sweet-breads on the fire in one quart of cold water, in which are mixed one tea-spoonful of salt and one table-spoonful of vinegar. When the water boils, take them off, and throw them into cold water, leaving them until they get cold; now lard them with lardoons about one-eighth of an inch square and two inches long. Chop rather fine one-third of a medium-sized onion (one ounce), four or five slices of carrot (one and a half ounces), half a stalk of celery, and one sprig of parsley. Put in the bottom of a baking-dish trimmings of pork; on this place the sweet-breads, and sprinkle the chopped vegetables over the top; bake them twenty minutes in a hot oven. Cut a slice of bread into an oval or any fancy shape, and fry it in a *sauté* pan in a little hot butter, coloring it well; put this *croûton* in the centre of a hot platter, on which place the sweet-breads. Serve pease or tomato-sauce around.

SWEET-BREAD FRITTERS.

Parboil the sweet-breads as before explained, and cut them into slices about half an inch thick; then sprinkle over them pepper and salt, a little grated nutmeg, some finely chopped parsley, and a few drops of lemon-juice; dip them each into French fritter batter   fry them a moment in boiling-hot lard. Always test the lard before frying by putting in a piece of bread or a bit of the batter; if it turns yellow readily, it is hot enough. Drain them well; pile them on a napkin neatly arranged on a platter; garnish them with fried parsley, *i. e.*, parsley thrown into the lard, and skimmed out almost immediately.

Sweet-bread Croquettes (*New York Cooking-school*).

After two pairs of sweet-breads are blanched (boiled in salted water as described), cut them into dice; cut also half a box (four ounces) of mushrooms into dice. Make a *roux* by putting one and a half ounces of butter into a saucepan, and when it bubbles sprinkle in two ounces of flour; mix and cook it well; then pour in a gill of strong stock or cream; when this is also mixed, add the dice, which stir over the fire until they are thoroughly heated; take them from the fire, add the beaten yolks of two eggs, which return to the fire a moment to set, without allowing to boil. When cool, form into *croquettes*; roll them first in cracker-crumbs, then in egg, then in cracker-crumbs again, and fry them in boiling lard.

The *croquettes* may be cone-shaped, with a stick of parsley or celery pressed in the top for a stem just before serving; or the sweet-bread *croquettes* may be made in the same manner as chicken *croquettes* (French cook receipt), substituting sweet-breads for the chickens. They may be served alone, or with pease, or with tomato or Bechamel sauce, etc.

Skewer of Sweet-breads.

Parboil the sweet-breads as before described; cut them into slices or scollops about half an inch or more thick; sprinkle them with pepper and salt, and egg and bread-crumb them; now run a little skewer (see page 56) through two of these slices, alternating with two thin, square slices of bacon; fry in boiling lard; serve a tomato or cream sauce in the centre, and garnish with parsley. Serve one skewerful to each person at table.

MUTTON.

The best roasts are the leg, the saddle, and the shoulder of mutton. They are all roasted according to the regular rules for roasting. In England, mutton is hung some time before cooking. There must be something in the air of England quite different from that of America in reference to the hanging of meats and game; there, it is to be confessed, the mutton, after having hung a certain length of time, certainly is most delicious; here it would be unwholesome, simply not fit to eat. These joints of which I speak are also good braised. Serve currant-jelly-sauce with the roast, or garnish it with stuffed baked tomatoes.

Boiled Leg of Mutton.

This should be quite fresh. Put it into well-salted boiling water, which do not let stop boiling until the meat is thoroughly done. The rule is to boil it a quarter of an hour for each pound of meat. Caper-sauce should be served with this dish, either in a sauce-boat or poured over the mutton; garnish with parsley.

Mutton Cutlets.

Trim them well, scraping the bones; roll them in a little melted butter or oil, season, and broil them; or they are nice egged, bread-crumbed, and fried. They are especially nice when broiled, served around a bed of mashed boiled potatoes: the cutlets help to season the potatoes, which in turn well suit the meat. Tomato-sauce is also a favorite companion to the cutlets. They may, however, be served with almost any kind of vegetables, such as pease or string-beans, in the centre of the dish, and the cutlets arranged in a circle around.

Ragouts (*made of Pieces of Mutton, Veal, Beef, or Rabbits*).

Cut the upper parts, or the neck, from a fore-quarter of mutton (or take inferior cuts from any part) into pieces for a ragout; heat a heaping table-spoonful of drippings, or lard, in a saucepan, and when hot *sauté* in it the pieces of mutton (say two pounds) until they are almost done; take them out, put in a table-spoonful of flour, brown it, add at first a little cold or lukewarm water, mix it well, then add a quart of boiling water; now add also salt, Cayenne pepper, two cloves, the pieces of *sautéd* meat, three or four onions (not large), and six or seven peeled potatoes. Some prefer to boil the potatoes a few minutes in other water first, as the water in which potatoes are boiled is considered unwholesome; cover the stew-pan well. When the vegetables are cooked, take them and the meat out, skim off every particle of fat from the gravy, taste to see if it is properly seasoned, pour it over the ragout, and serve.

These ragouts can be made with the neck, or any pieces of veal, in the same manner, or with pieces of beef, in which case carrots might be substituted for the potatoes. A ragout of rabbits is most excellent made in the same way, adding a glassful of red wine when it is almost done.

In buying a fore quarter of mutton, there are enough trimmings for a good ragout, with a shapely roast besides.

Another Ragout (*of Pieces of Mutton, Veal, Beef, etc.*).

Make rich pie-paste about the size of an egg (for four persons); roll it a quarter of an inch thick; cut it into diamonds, say an inch long and half an inch broad. Bake them, and put them aside until five minutes before serving the ragout. Take mutton, veal, beef, or almost any kind of meat. Any cheap cut of meat will make a good ragout, and choice cuts had better be cooked in other ways. In this instance, I will say, cut two pounds from the side of mutton. Put a table-spoonful of lard or drippings into a saucepan, and when hot *sauté* in it the pieces of mutton; when half done, place them in a kettle. Add a heaping table-spoonful of flour to the drippings in the saucepan; stir it constantly several minutes to brown, then add gradually a pint of hot water; now pour this over the meat in the kettle, adding three small onions, two sprigs of parsley, three cloves, and a clove or bulb of garlic, if you have it; pepper and salt. Cover it closely, and let it simmer slowly for an hour, occasionally turning the kettle to one side to skim off all the fat. Five minutes before serving, add the diamonds of crust.

At the moment of serving, take out the meat, crust, and three onions, and arrange them on a hot platter. Pass the gravy through a sieve, and skim off every remaining particle of fat; taste to see if it is properly seasoned with pepper and salt, and pour it over the meat.

Sheep's Tongues, with Spinach.

Braise a number of sheep's-tongues with salt pork, parsley, onion, some whole peppers, a tea-spoonful of sugar, and enough stock to cover them. Let them simmer one and a half hours. Serve with spinach in the centre of the dish, and seasoned with lemon-juice, a little of the tongue stock, some Cayenne pepper, salt, and butter. Serve the tongues around it, and diamonds or fancy cuts of fried bread (*croûtons*) around the outside circle.

SHEEP'S TONGUES À LA MAYONNAISE.

Boil half a dozen sheep's tongues with one or two slices of bacon, one carrot, one onion, two cloves, two or three sprigs of parsley, salt and pepper (some add two table-spoonfuls of sherry or port wine, but this may be omitted), and enough boiling water (or, better, stock) to cover them. Let them simmer about one and a half hours, replenishing the boiling water or the stock when necessary. When thoroughly done, skin and trim them neatly; lay them between two plates, to flatten them. A professional cook would glaze them with the stock boiled down in which they were cooked; however, this is only for the sake of appearance. Arrange them in a circle around a dish, with a *Mayonnaise* sauce poured in the centre.

SHEEP'S TONGUES, WITH SAUCE TARTARE.

Boil the tongues in salted water into which has been squeezed the juice of half a lemon (for six tongues). Serve with *sauce Tartare*

Milton Keynes UK
Ingram Content Group UK Ltd.
UKHW050640221123
432980UK00014B/770